10647348

What the Church of God Means to Me

by
**Dan Harman
and Friends**

Warner Press, Inc.
Anderson, Indiana

Copyright ©1990 by Warner Press, Inc.
ISBN 0-87162-600-4   Stock #D8855
All Rights Reserved
Printed in the United States of America
Warner Press, Inc.

Arlo F. Newell, Editor in Chief
Dan Harman, Book Editor
Richard Willowby, Editor
Cover by Larry Stuart

Contents

SO WHAT'S THIS
BOOK ALL ABOUT?

Yes, it's a series of stories, experiences, and revelations by a beautiful corp of plain people who love the Church of God. Sometimes their place of worship carries a sign that says "Community Church" or "Church of the Foothills" or "Church at the Crossing," but they have the same heritage.

No, you won't be mired down with doctrine. If you want history and teachings and theological foundations, we've added a page or so in the back.

Yes, this is a feeling book. My friends and I feel deeply about our church. We feel so deeply that one day I asked myself, If I were a person new to the Church of God, what would I want to know about the church? Maybe your answer is different from mine, but I'd want to know about the people, the activities, and how those people felt about their church—how they related to it, and how they felt about each other.

So, if you want the perspective of second generation Church of God people, here it is. Whatever you think of what my friends and I have brought together, remember: right where you are, you will most likely find a congregation of the Church of God with people who think and feel and remember just about as my friends and I do. Get to know them.

Mingle among them. Dare to ask one or two of them, "What do you think about the Church of God?" My guess is that you'll be pleasantly surprised at the joy, the warmth, the love that shows on their faces as they respond. You'll probably come up with an experience that should have been included in this book.

All right: check out the Church of God and write your own book on it. As you get to know the Church of God, I firmly believe you'll discover some deeply entrenched feelings that will stir you and whet your soul's appetite for more. It is not perfect, but it is miles ahead of anything else I have ever come upon, this Church of God I love.

Friends: join my friends and take a look at what this church means to us. I really think you'll like the experience.

Dan Harman
Anderson, Indiana 1990

"Jesus dealt with what God labels as proper life for [human beings]. He dealt with the human situation, with how [people] mishandle themselves and mistreat each other, with the need of every [person] to break free from selfishness and live for God."
—James Earl Massey[1]

The man who bases his life on Christ's teachings, however, has both the Father and Son as his God.
—2 John 9, J. B. Phillips

1

THE DREAM

The dream: the magnificent, simplistic, idealistic dream—that soaring call to reproduce the New Testament concept of pure Christianity. No sects, no creeds, no denominational barriers, no competition, and certainly no membership lists. The Church of God dream. The vision of reformation. The dream of pulling together all God's people into one grand and glorious church, one church with unity, love, and power. The old-timers had it. A hundred years ago the "saints" who later became identified as Church of God people believed that just such a Christian community could be formed and could live and grow and encompass the Christian world.

History will have to evaluate how close we have come to this ideal.

But in any survey of what the Church of God means to people today you'll have to face the fact that Christian doctrine has been a powerful and effective force in drawing individuals and families to the Church of God. What we believe has come to be central in the hearts of many people.

"I liked baseball," said Cliff Tierney, "but when I tried to join the team in Cleveland, I found that I had to attend church to be a member." Cliff made the team. The more he learned about the church and what it stood for, the more he was attracted. "I liked the idea that I didn't need a middle person to have communion with Jesus." Salvation and church membership were one.

Cliff "earned" his way to youth camp as a teen-ager by memorizing fifty Bible verses. Camp introduced Cliff to what has always been at the heart of Church of God emphasis: Bible doctrine. Doctrine and love combined for Cliff. As adults, Cliff and his wife, Betty, were brought into the church family by the love and dedication of Pastor John Neal. ("He helped me fix my car after Betty fixed him biscuits and gravy," is the way Cliff explains it.)

The Church of God stands for something—not a fuzzy general Christianity, but truth that comes from the Bible and truth that can be preached and practiced with fervor and love. So many people across America have said, "What impressed me about the atmosphere of the Church of God service was that these people meant what they said, what they sang."

Clarence McGillen is remembered in Johnson City, Tennessee, by the old-timers there for a series of dramatic confrontations with the movie houses of the day. In one, McGillen, pastor of Tacoma Church of God, was furious about a life-size cardboard cutout of a near-naked woman, standing in front of a theater to advertise the latest film. "Not in my town," he said and tore the cutout to bits. To believe meant to take action.

Salvation, the infilling and ministry of the Holy Spirit, healing, the unity of the church, and a dozen other Bible-based teachings have always been precious to Church of God people.

In many quarters today the specialty of Christian groups often seems to be all-inclusiveness concerning doctrine. The Church of God has a simple stand along these lines: we accept all people but do not endorse all doctrine. To be sincere, to accept the Bible as a rule of faith, and to live for Christ are central necessities. But the uniform interpretation of doctrine is not a requirement for fellowship.

How well I recall a home-visit to a Christian woman who had worshiped with us for many years. In asking about her faith, I was amazed to hear her say, "Yes, I love Jesus. He has saved me. I believe I will go to heaven when I die," I smiled. She continued, "and when I am reincarnated and come back to earth again, I know I will be a better person." She had some counseling to look forward to, but I couldn't doubt her sincerity or her faith in Christ.

Another surprising interpretation of doctrine comes from Arizona. A marvelous Church of God woman bought a wood-burning cookstove during World War I. As the years went by, the stove performed beautifully. In due time the main grate that held the wood in place broke in two. In spite of all the woman's attempts to replace it, no replacement could be found; she lacked money for a new stove and the baked goods that were produced kept looking worse and worse.

In a bedtime prayer, one of the children prayed, "Dear Lord, please heal our stove." The whole family stands ready to testify that the next morning the grate was welded together without human hands touching it. No one could find an answer other than God's honoring the childlike prayer.

4

Orpha O. DuBois still remembers the wonderful combination of "hard-nosed doctrine" and real love. The morals and ethics preached in her childhood stuck with her. ("I remember wiggling my toes in the sawdust of the camp meeting tabernacle and finding a penny. My problem was whether the penny was mine or the Lord's since I found it in God's house?")

"But such thoughts were balanced beautifully as the saints all hugged me and transmitted their real love for me week by week. Often the pastor would give me a big handshake, just like the grown-up people."

In every community where the Church of God has taken root you'll find folks to whom the old *Gospel Trumpet* magazine was crucial to their faith. Laura Benson Withrow tells about "growing up with a *Gospel Trumpet* in my hands."

She's not an old-timer, but she tells of her early years: "The Church of God was knit into the fiber of my being at birth." But this close tutorage wasn't like that of a cult. "I did not chafe under the sometimes strict behavioral codes of those years." She went on to attend Anderson University and marry a pastor, and today she enjoys a rich life of service and ministry.

Thousands of people around the world have come to love the Church of God because of its doctrines. Yes, we know what the surveys say:

- How does this church minister to my whole family?
- Are the people friendly, is the pastor "attractive?" Other survey results help determine the programs of local congregations. But at the heart, at some point, the sincere seeker must ask, "But what do you believe, really believe?"

A tiny woman, full of vigor and spunky energy once said to her husband, "Let's go to another church today." He agreed and purely by chance ("It wasn't chance. God did it," she says) their car got onto the wrong street and ended up in front of a Church of God building.

"The pastor preached a sermon on doctrine," Helen Toner says. "We went back. It was more doctrine. Then slowly we began to see: people must experience a relationship with Christ before they can be part of God's family."

That's been at the heart of Church of God teaching from the very beginning. For years a slogan was circulated among our churches: "The church where Christian experience makes you a member." Knowing Christ, being accepted by him, makes you part of the Church of God—and it works. For humans to decide the basis for acceptance opens the door to every form of prejudice and political activity. But to agree together that, when a person is accepted by Christ, that person then is automatically accepted by the church, brings common sense and hope.

From time to time a variety of doctrinal emphases have been promoted in the Church of God. For awhile one of the early leaders, F. G. Smith, toured the nation (and the world) with charts to illustrate the Bible Book of Revelation. Debates, variations, and downright differences accompanied his interpretation.

In another era the outward appearance of true Christians was defined closely, all by Bible doctrines—as the prophets of that day interpreted them. Coffee and tea, neckties, beads, curled hair, and a host of other outward signs of inner spirituality were debated. Then the emphasis shifted to another portion of God's Word.

The Church of God began with strong doctrinal convictions. Some seem off-center as we look back. Few of us agree with the historic shifts of concern or the interpretations frequently expounded among Church of God leaders, but I love the concentration on basics, the love for the deeper matters of the faith.

In my life, my personal interpretation of Bible truths has always been at the heart of my spiritual life: not the program, the buildings, or the pastors I've known, and I am thrilled to realize that this personal faith is treasured all across the Church of God. We believe in our Lord, not the institutions or the traditions or the hierarchy. Our personal faith is central, and in the Church of God this has always been honored. That means a great deal to many of us. The methods or the heros or the buildings or institutions do not matter in the end. Our faith, our convictions matter.

I like that in the Church of God. I think that what my friends and I are trying to say is this:

1. Doctrinal convictions are fundamental. We shun the title *Fundamentalist*; but personal, doctrinal convictions are basic concerns with us.

2. The teachings of the church are from the Bible, but measuring our success in living them is not always easy.

3. To be a Christian is to be saved, acceptable to God. Church membership is based on this simple idea: if we are acceptable to God, we must accept each other as sisters and brothers in Christ.

4. Doctrine isn't worth much unless we live it out in daily life.

5. While some people have odd convictions, Church of God people in general are tolerant of such beliefs.

6. Moral strictness, tough ethical standards,

and high morals are part of the way of life for Church of God people.

These friends helped with Chapter 1:

Cliff Tierney	Helen Toner
Clarence McGillen	James Earl Massey
Laura Withrow	Orpha O. DuBois
Inez C. Cobb	

A Quote to Leave With You:

"People keep talking about great ideas, brilliant questions and the problems of God's existence. But we're hungry for you, Jesus, not ideas or theories."

—Anonymous

"The love of God and loyalty to the Church of God has given me a precious treasure of life-long friends."
—Inez C. Cobb[2]

By this all men will know
that you are my disciples, if
you love one another.

—John 13:35

2

THE LOVE, THE FRIENDS, THE FEELINGS

Handshakes are easy. Ask any politician. A smile, a hello, and a firm handclasp—you see it in church gatherings all the time. But love is something more.

Bud and Birdie were a lovely couple. Each had Christian backgrounds, but in 1952 Bud's parents had invited them to a "new" church: the Church of God.

The words etched in stone said it all: "A Church of Stone with a Heart of Love." The Smiths had found a home church for life.

But in eighteen months Birdie's world collapsed; after a bout with cancer Bud was gone. Greg and Ron were young; Randy was a tiny tot. But Birdie, her in-laws ("adopted parents" Birdie calls them), and a beautiful family of Church of God people all put their hands in the hands of God, and they came out triumphant, happy, and very much in love with the Lord and his church.

In the meantime, Birdie found Don (or was it to be credited to God, God's friends, and the church itself?).

The congregation prophesied the new union. "Our constant togetherness in church with the congregation warmly teasing and cheering us on, eventually led to marriage."

Does the Church of God mean something special to Birdie? Ask her. I know what she'll say.

"The Church of God has been God's instrument in my life to provide a spiritual cradle to be the nurture of my faith—the altar where the most profound changes in my life have taken place, and the path by which God has led me through very deep waters and over mountain tops to find a closer walk with him."

She's actually identifying real love. Something a lot more than a smile and handshake.

Birdie discovered God's love in the Church of God as an adult. Many of us get a bit teary-eyed when we think of having known this cocoon of love all our days.

As a tot Jeannette loved sitting in the worship services where people sang from a book with a "jumble of notes and letters on the page that made no sense at all to a five-year-old child." (They sat—as many families do—on the back row with the little ones, so they could slip out more easily if the children became too restless.)

"The hymnal made no sense. But what did make sense was the obvious joy and happiness that seemed to fill every space in that sanctuary." The songs of love especially impressed her.

"I may have been a five-year-old in my father's arms, but the whole congregation was telling me the story of God's love for me when they sang of the Good News of Jesus Christ."

Once in a while I visit a congregation where the children are assigned space in a cold, damp basement (fewer and fewer do this today). Righteous indignation starts rising in my system. The little ones are so vital, so central to the church. They deserve the best.

Not many such congregations are left anymore. Time and again I am impressed by the creative, exciting, attractive ways that the gospel of Christ, the Bible, the church itself is taught to the little ones. At the heart of course is the vision.

Clair Shultz has given a lifetime of service to the Church of God, mainly in the field of missions work. How did it start?

"The Lima, Ohio, saints took an interest in our younger clan—three small boys, of which I was the youngest—and helped us to find love and a place of fellowship in the church. In many ways I got anchored into the church when I was young. The Church of God gave me my training and got me ready for college (a Church of God college) when I was eighteen."

The story can be repeated over and over. In my own life, I recall vividly the warmth, the glow, the love, and the people in whom I had absolute trust as a child. I didn't know of any problems in the church family. Doctrinal struggles were pushed back so that the spirit of love could be seen as paramount. Paul's high spot for love (1 Corinthians 13) should be evident in week-to-week church life. The little ones deserve this. The adults must live it to be genuine.

"Friends for a lifetime" is a favorite phrase for our family. It continually surprises me at how many of these have come from my early years in the Church of God nest. As a tot they hugged me. As a teen they tolerated the smart-alek. As a budding pastor they overlooked the sharp edges. Church of God people who nurture the young ones need a special spot near the throne when Christ comes again.

Working in a bookstore can be a boring, dull, heavy chore for most people. Of course, for those who love to read it is a boundless treasure chest of joy. Evelyn felt that joy when she worked at "The Book Store" (beautifully generic, isn't it?) in Johnson City, Tennessee. One day she read a book published by Warner Press. She was so impressed that she began reading the data on the author listed on the back. To her surprise the author was a pastor in her town.

Next Sunday Evelyn and Rollins were in service at Johnson City's Tacoma Church of God, "We were impressed by the friendliness of the people, specially the two or three who came each week to visit us in our new home. I felt comforted to know they cared so much. We kept attending. We learned the beliefs. There we discovered the simple truth that our personal belief in the saving power of Christ was at the heart of the church.

"Through the years that have followed (twenty now) we have found true brotherhood in times of happiness as well as in troubled times. We are grateful. It started with genuine love, honestly offered."

Visiting various congregations of the Church of God will do anyone good as vacations and business trips take you across the country. Each one seems to have a different flavor, a different beat. I risk my reputation when I encourage this. You may very well find congregations you just don't like. But try them anyhow. I believe you'll appreciate the love and the creative ways different groups have in expressing this love.

There's the Shenandoah Homes Church of God, a spinoff of Shenandoah Homes Retirement Village in Roanoke, Virginia. A few years ago Sheri Little worked there as a summer intern.

"The congregation is made up of people who come from various religious backgrounds. Convenience is a big factor in why they attend church services at Shenandoah, but it is not the major factor. People come there because they want to. The major pull is the Christian love and acceptance they feel when they worship. The people practice being the family of God.

"The love is evident," says Sheri. "They see themselves as the body of Christ. Commitment is big. They come with canes, on walkers, in wheelchairs. But they come, and together they find the love of Christ among the group.

"Shenandoah is an example of how it is possible for Christians from different backgrounds to worship God in a beautiful way."

Some congregations specialize in singles ministry, some in small group diversity. But I have found love in each one. That is why I recommend touring among the churches.

The wind whipped up, the funnel cloud zoomed in, and in a flash Nancy Wood of Vinita, Oklahoma, found herself and her family out in the cold. The tornado left them homeless. "I had to write to you," she explains. "If your book is to tell people what the Church of God is all about, then you have to know this." Nancy is a woman who is sold on the Church of God.

"From the first time we attended, we felt the warmth and total acceptance of the people," Nancy says, "and these things are a rarity in today's world."

When the tornado hit, Nancy didn't know what to do. "Then the people of the First Church of God pitched in—donations, work, tools, labor. Anything needed was provided. Without their help, we'd still be freezing in that small, drafty summer camper," Nancy notes.

You can see her smile across the miles: "For all those years we knew how wonderful they were, and then when that tornado hit, we found out how terrific they are in a time of crisis.

"I've found a small piece of heaven right here on earth."

Friendship, love, acceptance: how else do you express the heartfelt feelings that Church of God people have for each other? I've seen the demonstrations of caring. They are more than a handclasp. Of course there are people I can't feel close to; close friendships are made carefully, over the years. But my best friends seem always to emerge from the church family. Funny, I guess I'd do all I could for many of them if they'd ask.

Friendship and love go hand in hand in the Church of God.

May I add a personal note? Love took a special form for my wife and me at our wedding. Herschell Rice performed the ceremony. He did a fine job. But the moment that stands out in my memory is that moment on the day before our wedding, when we walked into the room that was to be used for the reception.

There, on hands and knees with scrub brush and bucket nearby, was Pastor Rice. "The cleaning lady couldn't work today, and I thought you ought to have a shiny clean floor," he said, a bit embarrassed that he had been caught in this practical display of love and concern. You just don't forget examples of love like that.

Like we've said before, surely there is love and care and concern in many churches of different denominational loyalty all around the world. They serve the same Christ who is worshiped in Church of God congregations.

I've seen the love in our churches. It means something to me. It gives me joy and pride and a warm feeling of security—and from my experience these are feelings hard to come by in our world.

There is no way I can summarize the church as a business or a force or an army. I know all these terms apply at times. But for me the church is a family, a loving family. It's an older woman encouraging my wife as she fearfully walked into the role of pastor's wife. It is a godly elder statesman of the church patiently enduring my foolish, rookie evaluation of "what the Church of God needs."

Love and concern brought the Stratners to the back of the church building at midnight to see the Harmans huddled on the floor when we'd been evicted from our little apartment "for having too much junk." The landlord was terribly prejudiced when he discovered that his new tenants were Protestant ministers. But love was what moved the Stratners to take us in and house us in their home till we could get another apartment.

Love digs in deeply when it strikes.

Love works wonders in the heart.

Love is the cement that holds the church together.

Being part of the Church of God family means a great deal to me, and I agree with Paul (1 Corinthians 13) when he makes love central in the Christian walk.

The Church of God is special to me because. . . .

1. That's where I found love that began with Jesus' love for someone.

2. The love that is launched in the church family—the Church of God family to me—stands the test of time—it lasts.

3. From the love in the church can stem all kinds of love for others: romance, fellowship, care and concern, deep friendships.

4. In some wonderful way, music in the church helps express feelings of love we often fail to express in simple conversation.

5. The Church of God cares for and loves children. They loved me and they love my children and my childrens' children.

6. The friendships I've found in the church family are anchored in real love—not business, sports, or any other human social function.

7. People outside the church can understand and respond to the friendship and love that Christians show forth.

8. Love that Christ inspires is willing to put itself out, to serve.

9. I've seen the Church of God respond to needs from a motive of love. I've not found that outside the church—pity, empathy, guilt, but not *agape* love.

10. The love that drew me into the church also drew in the woman whom God gave me for my wife. Thank you, God.

These people contributed to this chapter:

Nancy Wood	Carl Stradner
C. W. and Retha Shultz	R. C. Wilson
Birdie and Don Noffsinger	Jeannette Flynn
Rollins and Evelyn Justice	Herschell Rice
Sheri Little	

A Thought to Take With You:

"Here is the truth in a little creed,
Enough for all the roads we go:
In love is all the law we need,
In Christ is all the God we know."
—Edwin Markham[3]

"Bill has a strong conviction that when you're given something, you are also given a responsibility. His life has been driven by that."
—Gloria Gaither[4]

"Sing a new song to the Lord telling about his mighty deeds! . . . The whole earth has seen God's salvation of his people. . . . Make a joyful symphony before the Lord, the King! . . . Let the earth and all those living on it shout, 'Glory to the Lord.' "
—from Psalm 98,
Living Bible

3

THE SINGING CHURCH

Many Sandi Patti stories are going around these days; she's one of the all-time top stars of gospel music and her Church of God heritage is well-known.

One day Sandi was signing autographs in the beautiful Christian Book Store in her own hometown when a young girl, about first-grade age, stepped up and presented her album to be autographed. The child had stars in her eyes. With a stammering voice, she blurted out, "Sandi, I love you. Last Halloween I even got all dressed up as Sandi Patti."

I am not sure just how the costume was designed, but it was clear who the girl idolized. Or, as another girl said, "I love Sandi because you can always count on her to sing songs that lift up Jesus. Some others are singing secular songs, but Sandi sings to the glory of God."

The Church of God has gained a most appropriate reputation for turning out top musicians. Barney Warren was a pioneer, but we still sing his stirring gospel songs. D. O. Teasley, D. S. Warner, and a host of others traveled this country with a Bible in one hand and a freshly written, singable gospel song in the other.

A faithful member of Park Place Church of God in Anderson, Indiana, Patti is joined by Bill and Gloria Gaither, Doug Oldham, and many others in keeping alive the tradition of excellent church music in the Church of God.

Can you sing? I can't. But we can each use our talents for Christ and the church. That is an encouragement to some of us who have poor singing voices. How thankful we all are for those beautiful people with their God-given talent for making sweet music.

Another thought impresses me: a number of simple people live undistinguished lives outside the circle of the church and yet are true giants in spiritual terms.

In my childhood "Mother MacDougal" was what some might call a "nobody" outside the church fellowship. But at times when she was with people, one or many, she beamed out the love of Christ in a marvelous way. Everyone relied on her counsel, trusted her judgment, and found in her a faithful and loving friend.

Another was "Brother Lawhon." I was so small that I never knew his complete name. His abilities were limited. However, Wednesday evening prayer meetings were alive with his testimonies of opportunities that God had given him to witness and help others. I might have thought he was bragging, except that my father often went around with Brother Lawhon, and he, too, told stories of the amazing way people responded to this crusty old navy veteran with arms full of tattoos and a testimony full of poor English.

Only in the fellowship of the church do some people shine.

The other day I listened to a tape of Herb Thompson, a veteran Church of God musician. Herb's outstanding voice and the way he uses it are uniquely suited to singing for the Lord.

When I was a child, Herb was the only soloist I ever wanted to hear sing. His story of learning how to sing while tending sheep out on the hillside fascinated me. With Lola at the piano and Herb hitting those high notes in the dramatic gospel ballads like "Zion's Hill" and the "Ninety and Nine," I sat transfixed service after service. No revival was ever complete to this kid unless the music was by Herb Thompson.

Bill and Gloria Gaither have made a lasting impression on the face of gospel music in this century. Most of us know them for the tremendously moving music, spectacular concerts, and exciting performances that attract thousands all through the year. Increasingly, Gloria is impressing us with the marvelous messages she shares from her heart, messages of poetry and prose without the music. The Gaithers are special.

But do you realize they are also active in the local church music of their home congregation? East Side Church of God in Anderson is "home," and the Gaithers give of themselves and their talents and time continually.

Another facet that ought to be known is the marvelous models the Gaithers are to the young people of the Anderson area. Recently Bill and Gloria were inducted into the Madison County, Indiana, Business Leaders Hall of Fame. "High time," you say? Yes, but the real impact is to know that one of the main functions of the Jaycees who sponsor this hall is that of Junior Achievement. The local newspaper described the worth of the salute to the Gaithers.

"The Gaithers, pioneers in the gospel music industry, did not set out to become entrepreneurs in the business world. They began as teachers whose love for music led them into singing and writing in their spare time. But as their songs caught on, they channeled their talents and efforts into a burgeoning career that now encompasses the Gaither Music Company, Alexandria House, Arios Publishing, Pinebrook Recording Studio, The New Gaither Vocal Band, Stage II Productions, and Jubilee Communications.

"The young men and women involved in Junior Achievement could ask for no better role models than Bill and Gloria."

Others call the Church of God "unique." Marthalene Kirby describes it: "We have services on Sunday morning, Sunday night, and Wednesday night just like the church around the corner, but that doesn't make us just a church among churches."

She lists some distinctives and concludes: "Music has been a great influence on my life. I started when I was ten. Mother would just call out a number from our church hymnal, and I'd start in right away singing or playing it on our home organ. I memorized about one-third of the songs in that old hymnal, words and music."

Marthalene's dad was a pastor, but she says, "I think the songs we sang taught me much more than my father's preaching." Now she lives right across the street from a Church of God campus and is so happy she can hardly stand it.

Want to play a mental game that can stagger the imagination? Try to picture a talent that God can't use in the church. Some of the most unusual skills ever dreamed of have come into practical use for God in his church.

Jesse Egly was an Electrolux sales representative. Naturally, his sales ability stood him in good stead in Church of God leadership; in addition to sales skills, "Papa Egly" was a great singer.

But God used another skill of his on at least two occasions. Surely others have done these things, but I had never heard of them before. In sales work, Electrolux people were trained to sell the equipment by emphasizing the low cost per week—not a total price for the equipment, but the cost per week to buy it on credit.

Jesse used it in the church. When time for a big missions offering came up, he simply went to the bank, borrowed the money he gave to the offering, then paid off the loan week by week throughout the year just as though it were a refrigerator.

When in the Great Depression the church needed some repairs and some coal, he simply went to the bank, mortgaged his home, and paid the church's debts. That's how he learned to conduct the world's business and so he might as well let God's work profit from what he'd learned. I like people like that. I like a church that produces people like Jesse.

Musicians singing, teachers teaching, and bankers managing the finances: these are natural.

Julia is one of the talented non-singers in the church and she has a unique gift. She loves people and has a marvelous, outgoing spirit about her. Her unique gift isn't her cooking (which is great—Danish) or her smile, as warm and wide as a sunny summer morning.

Julia saw a need and stepped in.

In working with the women of the Church of God, she noted that when a death occurred in the church family, the women were quick to step in and provide food. Julia helped.

But she also noted another need. Often the homes into which women took the food were all confused and out of order. Death brought a strange assortment of people into the home. The regular rhythm and system of the home were disrupted. No one seemed to be in charge. Simple tasks were being neglected.

So Julia decided, as quickly as she heard of a death in the church family, she packed her "kit" and drove to the home. With her wide smile, she presented herself at the door of the home that death had visited. "Hello. I'm here to help. Just show me where things go, and I'll take charge."

Now, I'm sure some people would respond negatively to such an intrusion. But I never met one. Julia would move in, from morning till night. She would quietly wash dishes, answer the phone, prepare food, make the beds, clean, smooth over differences among visitors, give advice (when requested only!), and in general do all those jobs a good hostess would do if a hostess were at her best.

At nighttime, when all the guests were gone, Julia made sure the home was in tip-top shape, then gathered her kit together and was off. This continued till after the funeral and the home got back to itself. What a challenge. What a ministry. How unique are the avenues of service that God brings to our minds when we let him. How I love the Church of God.

Music has a special place in the Church of God. Ron Patty has two deep loves in his active life (in addition to his wonderful family): sports and music. He rates them about equally, even though most of us would bow in awe of his skills as a musician.

"Carolyn and I both started out in church music very young. I sat in wonder at my sister's song leading in church, of my mother's piano playing, and of my dad's fine tenor voice. Carolyn was pushed into church playing when her pastor-dad needed help; she was only seven when she started as church pianist." Ron's wife, Carolyn, as well as three children, Sandi, Mike, and Craig, are dedicated lovers of church music.

Ron's ministry as both pastor and musician has etched strong feelings about church music into his heart. "You can reach people with a song who may never be touched by preaching." Indeed, one of the major concerns of all the concerts Ron and Carolyn have shared over the years is that of reaching out for people who wouldn't ordinarily be in church services.

"You take some poor guy whose wife has pressured him into coming to one of our concerts by promising it won't be anything like a church service and that's a challenge for us."

Chauncey Reece (see chapter 12) was pressured by his Christian wife into attending a Patty concert at Luke Air Force Base in Arizona. Chauncey, an airline pilot, was impressed with the quality music that Ron and Carolyn projected. So he tried a church service where Ron ministered. He liked it, too.

For some reason Ron thought Chauncey was a Christian. One Sunday after Reece had been attending a while, Ron asked, "How long have you been saved?" Chauncey didn't know what he was talking about. But he asked around. In just a few weeks, here he came down to the prayer room and in a few minutes Chauncey Reece was a Christian. Music was the key—Church of God music with a message.

"You can reach people with music," Ron says. "It is what I call the great door-opener. Long after we are gone out of town after a concert, the local pastor can start using the doors we've opened."

Music that is from the heart grabs you. Ron tells of a concert Sandi Patti was giving in Columbus, Ohio. She sang her heart out and after one touching song the cheers and applause rang out. When the cheers died down, Sandi came to the edge of the stage to sing, but before she could, a tiny voice called out. As Sandi looked down she saw a small girl in a wheelchair looking up at her. The tiny voice repeated to a hushed audience: "We love you, Sandi."

With a catch in her voice and a tear in her eye Sandi echoed back, "And we love you, too." The burst of applause told Sandi and the world that the crippled child spoke for all of them.

What talents can a child exhibit? Singing? Yes, lots of Church of God children sing beautifully to the glory of God. My son, "Tommy," could sing. But how well I recall a time when he launched out into an area of witness that brought tears to my eyes.

Tommy (it's "JT" now) gave his heart to

Christ when he was very young. From time to time, when I was preaching in one of the surrounding towns, he'd go along with me.

Pastor J. B. Chapman asked me to come and preach the gospel to the congregation at Church Hill, Kentucky. Night after night I preached and Tommy sat on the front row with a large contingent of other children.

One evening several of the children came forward to accept Christ. As the song was sung, other children came. Finally, Tommy stood all alone in the front row. All his friends were praying to accept Christ, a step he'd taken some time before.

The next evening as I came into the building, several people came to me and shook my hand: "Pastor Harman, you have a wonderful son." I wondered what they were talking about, so on the drive home that night, I asked Tommy.

"What happened last night that the people were so impressed by you?"

He was silent for a moment and then said, "I don't know, unless it was what I did at the door." I asked what that was.

"Well, when you all were singing at the end of the service, all the other guys were at the altar. I was already a Christian, but when I looked around, everyone was looking at me like I didn't love Jesus. So I went to the front door after the service and shook hands with everyone who went out and told them I was a Christian—just so they'd know."

I've often wondered if I would have had

the zeal to do that when I was Tommy's age. Witnessing is a talent God can use. J. T. loves the Church of God, and so do I.

Did you catch the theme of these stories?
1. God has beautifully called some outstanding people to serve him and the church with music.

2. Appearances can be deceiving: God sees the heart and can use even those the world feels are untalented.

3. The music heritage of the Church of God is rich.

4. Many of the music leaders we love are outstanding, even by the secular world's standards.

5. God uses any skill, once we commit it to him.

6. Music can reach people for Christ when they haven't been touched by preaching.

These friends shared from their hearts:

Jesse and Ida Egly	Herb Thompson
"Sister MacDougal"	"Brother Lawhon"
Bill and Gloria Gaither	Marthalene Kirby
J. T. Harman	Julia Steffensen
J. B. Chapman	Ron and Carolyn Patty
Sandi Patti Helvering	

A Quote to Think About
"Lord, give us ideas we never had before, so that alleluia and gloria and amen are like the experiences we know in daily life."
—Herbert Brokering[5]

"It struck me with great force that in the (Church of God) reformation movement there is a tremendous spiritual freedom. Thank God for the truth."

—Kenneth L. Crose[6]

If the Son sets you free, you
will be free indeed.
      —John 8:36 (NIV)

TOGETHER AND FREE

Ever get tired of the big buildup, the big
sell, the hype about the latest gadget on TV?
Me too. But then tactics, strategy, image are
popular considerations—even in churches.
Almost anything can be sold if it is packaged
and presented in the most attractive way.

Minnie S. Kelly said something you ought
to hear. She loves the Church of God. Why?
"Because it affords me the opportunity to
worship God in a quiet, reverent atmosphere—no attention-getting tactics, no pressure."

People who come to services at Church of

God buildings have a sense of freedom that appeals to me.

But remember, Minnie, the lack of an obvious strategy doesn't mean there isn't one. The freedom we feel in the Church of God is a marvelous blessing: we are free to interpret the Bible as we feel God intended, free to witness, pray, worship, and serve as God inspires. No person is boss over any other person in the Church of God.

We're free.

But we're not loose. We're not disorganized, confused, or at cross purposes with each other.

All of us need to keep in mind one aspect of freedom and unity. In the Bible (Acts 20:28 specifically) the phrase church of God is used. Notice that the word *church* begins with a small *c*. We believe that every Christian on earth, every person who has been reconciled to God, each one who has responded to Christ's call and has given her or his life to the Savior is in the one true church: the church of God (small *c*).

The Church of God (capital C) is a group with a history, institutions, programs, cooperative ministries, clergy, and property. (Check the section, *If You'd Like to Know More*, for a list of sources where you can find all the information you need.)

Now those of us in the Church of God are part of the church of God. That's simple enough, isn't it? We're not the whole thing by a long shot. But we're part of it.

We're free of human control but dedicated to being controlled by God. That's why the freedom we have isn't chaos. Over the years we've evolved some ministries that we feel God wants us to share with him. Without pressure, but cooperatively, we get together and try to get the job done.

This freedom works hand in hand with a strong sense of being united with all other Christians. Unity is another big word in the Church of God, but terribly tricky to define and illustrate. The responsibility that freedom always brings drives us to work together, to cooperate, sometimes to get behind ministries that honestly aren't our own number one priority.

But in order to get the job done, we work together, and from that feeling of working together, another word comes to the top—*togetherness.*

Now that's not a new word to you. Everybody uses it today. Family togetherness, corporate togetherness, fraternal togetherness. Sometimes we almost smother on it.

Spiritually there are several kinds of togetherness. Inner togetherness is important: getting our act together, making sense of daily living, putting our lives in order—a vital facet for each Christian.

For one, I fought that fight. Growing up in the Church of God, I experienced many church-related pressures. Outside, the world around me pulled its way. I was a disorganized mess. I needed inner togetherness.

When I finally got serious about my spiritual unity, I looked around. I didn't get in a hurry. Each day I'd watch the people I admired: teachers, neighborhood boys older than myself, parents, public heros. My insides must have been like my mother's when she first got up in the morning. I can see her now: seated on the edge of the bed, yawning, stretching, and just sitting there. If we looked at her, she'd say, "Just give me a minute to sit here and get myself together."

Thank God, I got myself together; rather, God got hold of me and with God's help, my spirit got headed in a single direction.

Togetherness rates high in the church family. Sometimes we experience it in social events, sometimes working parties or quilting hours, and sometimes in crying spells when God ministers to a needy person or group.

Wonderful women like Eleanor Newcomb of Madera, California, are known across the nation for an open house policy for traveling clergy, much like the early days when staying in hotels was unknown. Men and women of the Church of God know Eleanor as a marvelous, thoughtful breath of joy. She, and her husband, Elvin, have intertwined their lives with a great number of people.

My own home and the homes of hundreds of PK families (for the uninstructed, *PK* is a universal abbreviation for that odd, privileged clan of preachers' kids) were host to evangelists, professors, missionaries, and musicians who traveled across the country sharing their talents and message with local congregations.

A wide dimension of fellowship and togetherness needs to be highlighted: the fellowship out beyond the local congregation. Most of us look forward to the warm friends we meet in worship on Sundays, but wherever you go you can find Christian friends in other communities, even around the world.

International togetherness is often a warm and beautiful plus to Christian travelers. In 1987 the Church of God held an international World Conference in Seoul, Korea. Probably everyone who attended it embraced memories for a lifetime.

To Jody and Anne Hill the trip from West Virginia and back was something of a test of faith and togetherness.

"In the first service representatives of many nations paraded their countries' flags," Jody said. "My pride swelled. I was proud to be an American. But more, I was proud I was a Christian. I had something in common with everyone there. We all loved God, regardless of all the obvious differences between us."

The trip included Jody's bleeding ulcer attack and all the ways God arranged for perfect strangers to care for Jody. A pastor-friend helped; an Italian doctor helped; an interpreter appeared; surprisingly the hospital room had a TV with an English language channel.

God even came through with practical togetherness when the hospital bill came. The amount was low, but the emergencies had

41

cut short Jody's cash and no bank was available. The age-old practice of "passing the hat" brought in the needed funds.

Ann writes: "Jody grew stronger. So did our faith. We experienced what it meant to have no one but God to turn to. But we found that God knows who to send when we have needs. Even across the world the church is our family." Jody recovered and the Hills headed back to West Virginia with a renewed love for the church around the world.

An element of togetherness that you may have seen is cooperation among different congregations and pastors. Most Church of God groups work well with other groups who have the same dreams, the same goals, the same dedication to following the direction of the Holy Spirit.

In the hills of Kentucky, in that beautiful God-inspired culture where simple things seem so necessary to daily well being, the little congregation of Caney holds services. Back in 1903 Brother Joe Lykins held a tent meeting in the community, preaching the simple truths of the early Church of God pioneers: unity, love, holiness, salvation.

When the meetings were concluded, the group of new Christians and those who agreed with the teachings Brother Joe stood for, gathered to hold a worship service. They had no building and asked a local pastor for permission to meet on Sunday afternoons in the congregation's building.

No way. So they met in a school building. This pastor who had refused them permission stopped in to visit a service to see what heretical doctrines were being proclaimed. He was so impressed with the sincerity and the Bible-centered preaching that he immediately reversed his attitude, walked to the front of the gathering, and openly apologized; he invited them to make the Methodist building their home till they could get one of their own.

From the start this small congregation was community-minded. All through the years it has stayed that way. Now, in these days of urban sprawl, rural Caney, Kentucky, is shrinking. A small group continues, without a regular pastor.

"But," says Edwin Benton, "the last full-time pastor we had was Roy Benton and when he died, the whole community came out for the funeral. And that funeral was conducted by all the pastors of the area from every denomination around. From beginning to end, Caney has practiced unity and togetherness."

Togetherness coupled with individual freedom is part of the charm of being in the Church of God. Or, as Minnie Kelly says, "I like this movement because it affords me the opportunity to worship God in a quiet, reverent atmosphere—no attention-getting tactics, no pressure."

I continually am amazed that so many of us love the Church of God so deeply and so sincerely but often for very different reasons. Togetherness impresses me, but Minnie's feeling of freedom likewise is special.

As different as the ear is from the foot, so church people are different, yet necessary and important.

Looking around me among minister-friends I see variety. Some specialize in counseling, some are great pulpit masters, some teachers, some administrators. This is, of course, scriptural (see Paul's writings in 1 Corinthians 12). But to see it in action is an awe-inspiring experience. Just when God needs a special woman or man for a specific situation, one seems to appear.

In my life I have felt the freedom to become what God wanted of me: to make decisions without outside pressure, to find a ministry where God could use me, to decide doctrine, style, and Bible interpretation for myself. All around me I have been touched by others to whom this special kind of freedom is so vital. Those of us who have grown up in the Church of God may not appreciate this freedom as much as those who have "seen the light" and come in later years to the Reformation Movement of the Church of God.

For years only a small portion of the Christian world has actually practiced the Bible ordinance of the washing of feet on any regular basis. Like so many other topics mentioned in the Bible, people have passed it by and—usually for cultural and esthetic reasons—decided that while they agree with the need for humility, they see no need to actually, physically, wash one another's feet.

Read John 13 and see if the tradition of the Church of God to wash feet—at least during Holy Week—isn't what Jesus intended.

A number of years ago I was asked to take charge of a half-hour TV show during Holy Week. In preparing for the contents of the time allotted, I decided simply to demonstrate the activities of Jesus and the disciples in the Upper Room just before the trial and crucifixion.

Step by step, I walked the audience through the events, conversation, and activities of Matthew 26, Mark 14, Luke 22, and John 13.

Afterward, to my amazement, many more people favorably commented about the washing of feet than anything else. Indeed, viewers appeared to feel as though they had suddenly discovered a new and wonderfully meaningful Christian celebration. Freedom to be and do what God directs often evolves into a togetherness across all barriers.

I like that in the Church of God (and in the *church* of God).

In Other Words . . .

1. The Church of God has a kind of freedom that allows for all kinds of personal interpretation.

2. This is coupled with an ongoing concern to get the work of Christ done, and much of this must be done by cooperating together.

3. As we get together, we enjoy the fellowship; we find that just being together in a variety of projects and for a variety of reasons is spiritually uplifting.

4. Togetherness can be on at least three levels: (a) inner oneness; (b) getting together as a local church family; spreading this out to the larger family of neighbors and Christians who worship in other congregations; (c) togetherness with Christians from all around the world, from all communions—togetherness with the church of God (church with a small *c*).

5. As we extend and share in the opportunities of freedom and the fellowship of togetherness, we find God is at work all around the world just as surely and as effectively as God is in our lives.

These friends were part of chapter 4:

Minnie S. Kelly	Elvin and Eleanor Newcomb
Edwin Benton	Katherine Willis
Jody and Anne Hill	

Let this sink in:

"We have grasped the mystery of the atom and rejected the Sermon on the Mount."

—Omar N. Bradley[7]

"Outreach includes derelicts, middle-class people, congressional leaders. That's what the Church of God means: no limits."
—Helen Durham Russell[8]

SERVING

Sacrificial serving impresses me.

To see people pour out their energies, their time, talents, and fortunes in the work of the Lord leaves me in awe.

Notice how many of these people seem absolutely ignorant of the tremendous sacrifice they are giving. The ones I've seen seem to be having the time of their lives.

Back in the early 1950s Ross Minkler was working with a dedicated team of church people to expand and develop Larchmont Church of God in Louisville. "Green Pastures" radio program was a vital part of the plan.

"Expansion" meant, of course, that the growing congregation needed larger worship space. "Only one way to expand the facilities," one trustee said, "but we can't do that. It would bring us too close to the apartment building next door. The city zoning forbids it."

That apartment building was owned by another trustee, Oscar Seidel, sitting across the table.

The silence around the room reflected the frustration everyone felt. If God wanted expansion, then why the obstacle? God—and Oscar Seidel—solved the dilemma.

"The city can't object if the church owns those apartments, can they?" With that Oscar sacrificed and sold the building to the church for the extremely low price he'd paid for it many years before.

Sacrificial service impresses me.

Lorraine Charlton has spent a lifetime attending Church of God services. "I haven't found anything better," she says and she's seen decades come and go.

She thought she'd seen everything till a fire destroyed the house of an aunt and uncle, killing them both. In that fire, Lorraine's eighty-five-year-old mother was forced out into the winter night where the wind factor and temperature hit seventy-five below zero.

"Mom lost practically all her possessions,

but the Church of God people took her in, and when the love and generosity ended, she owned more than she had before the fire." What a testimony. What a memory. What a church.

Many of the leaders through the years were not the officially ordained clergy, but lay pastors and gospel workers. My own father was fully ordained, yet recorded himself as a gospel worker rather than a minister or pastor. His sacrifice would fill another book.

Paul J. Bentley never applied for ordination. But in his years of ministry beginning in the 1930s, he raised up congregations, shepherded them, built them, and then turned them over to trained, ordained pastors.

"He never became a full-time pastor," son J. Grant Bentley says, "but he spent all his life as a minister." Preaching, building, personal witness, and a tremendous example cost Brother Bentley a great deal, but he had found his place of service and thousands cheer his profound contribution to their lives.

The dedication and sacrifice of Sunday school teachers and workers is known around the world. Many have given their whole lives to the classroom, without financial profits and often with little recognition.

Dave Sebastian is a Church of God pastor,

third generation Church of God. "My parents tell me that a church service was the first place I went when I left the hospital at birth."

But after serving in the army, Dave needed an adult introduction to the church. He found it in a Church of God Sunday school teacher's invitation to Dave and his bride, Debbie, to become part of a brand-new class for young marrieds, meeting in the church loft. "Bob and Iona Asher took on the task of teaching that class with fear and trembling."

It was what the Sebastians needed, what every young couple needs. "The contagious Christlike spirit of our teachers was a challenge. They got us into the Bible. With the Ashers, we were invited to visit other couples.

"Then the class started a Friday night Bible study and prayer time." To make a long story short, without the Ashers and their influence it is hard to say where some wonderful people would be today. "What we do know is that today five of those couples are in full-time Church of God ministry."

Influence is more than methods or exact wording or audio-visuals. The influence, over the years, of godly teachers can't be over-emphasized.

Ruth (Wolfe) Vanosdol has been such a teacher for over fifty years. She is "seen them come and go." From a long line of Church of God leaders, Ruth retains sweet and satisfying memories. "One of the best was to realize that some of my former students had gone into Church of God ministry of one sort or another. Steve and Cindy Shoop, for instance, were in my fourth-grade class in Sunday school. The picture of them leaving Dayton, Ohio, airport, heading out to Swaziland, Africa, as Church of God missionaries sticks with me."

Sometimes sacrifice comes in different shapes—no official title or position, no overtime hours in the church building. Dave and Donna Miller are like that. Their ministry is the care of tiny ones who are too crippled or too ill to be cared for in the homes of their parents, yet don't need constant hospital care. They carry on quite a ministry: demanding, eye-opening, taxing on energy and spirit.

They've cared for a number of pitiful shapes and sizes. But one small one sticks out: Amber, born of American Indian parents who deserted her. After all the care and supervision, Donna couldn't part with this one. "Let's adopt her," Donna pleaded, and so, today, if you visit the Church of God in San Bernardino, don't be surprised to see a sweetly smiling blonde woman, being pulled along by the cutest brunette with big black eyes and a smile that will melt your heart.

Please don't mention sacrifice to Dave and Donna, but that is an accurate term—sacrificial serving that makes life worthwhile. Amber may never know it took so much to give her a loving home, and the Millers see no reason to mention it.

Mariana was an inspiration to everyone who met her. Maybe that's why everyone was hit so hard when a stroke left her bedfast with major paralysis. Her age was against her, and in spite of everything the doctors could do, she ended up in a nursing home.

"Therapy, that's what she needs," husband Floyd said. He pushed and phoned and encouraged all he could. But no therapist could satisfy the quality care that Floyd wanted for his beloved Mariana.

So Floyd took over. He begged the use of an empty room near Mariana's room. He took his own blanket there and slept on the floor. Then, every hour or so, day and night, he got up, went across the hall and worked on Mariana. Fingers, arm, face, speech: every area that was affected got its share of attention.

She smiled. Slowly she moved a hand. Then some talking. Finally, she could feed herself. The word miracle was never used, but you could read it on the doctors' faces when they discharged Mariana into the care of her husband. "You can give her far more of what she needs than we can."

Sacrificial service, motivated by a great love—somehow it sounds like John 3:16, doesn't it?

When Keith O'Neil answered the phone he couldn't be prepared for the shock. "Your partner in business and his whole family were just killed in an auto wreck."

After all the necessary matters were cared for, Keith sat back and evaluated the situation. So many details had been left hanging, so many left undone—dreams his partner had, business deals to be completed.

In the midst of everything else that followed, a strange project got underway. An empty lot near where the wreck occurred slowly developed into a park: small, but beautiful and much needed. On his own, with little outside help, Keith has created a living memorial to his partner. He worked late into the night, early at dawn, sacrificing and building, all to keep a memory alive.

Someday you may stumble onto this park. It's called "Speicher Park." If you do, thank God for a Church of God builder who carried out the dreams of a partner he loved.

Church of God people often sacrifice for people they will never see again. A work camp to the interior of Guatemala a few years ago demonstrates this.

The group went to build a church building of concrete blocks in a tiny village. They fell in love with the people and spent a good deal of their time fellowshiping and counseling with the Church of God people they lived among.

Finally, word came that they would have to get to work on the building. They sent a rickety truck into town to get a load of concrete blocks. While the truck was gone, a sudden tropical downpour swelled the stream near the village and made the roads mud ruts.

When the truck returned, it stalled on the little wooden bridge over the stream, and as it tried to get started, the bridge gave way, dropping the truck with its load into the roaring stream. The driver was safe, but the truck was totaled, and every concrete block was ruined.

No time was left to find a truck, buy the blocks, and build the church building. Why hadn't they started sooner? Why had the truck wrecked? What would they do?

With downcast hearts they quickly built a wooden frame church building. With no great enthusiasm, they dedicated it, packed up, and went home.

In the next few years each camper often asked, "Why was our trip a failure—all our work, our saving, our sacrifices to make the trip. Why?"

Then came the terrible earthquake of the mid-1970s. The little town they'd worked in was at the epicenter of the quake. Every building made of concrete block ended up a pile of dust. When it was over a strange sight met the villagers' eyes. The Church of God stood proud and firm. It had swayed and shook, but all through the terrible shocks it stood fast.

In the weeks that followed word gradually leaked back to the work campers. "We know why you built a wooden building for us. Since the quake, it has been the food distribution center, the medical center, the government center for the whole territory. People flock here daily to pray and get to know the God we know, the God who even protects from the destruction of an earthquake."

Now, that may or may not have been the reason the wooden building was built instead of a concrete block building. But don't try to tell that to those people who gave all they had to do something they believed in, only to find that God seemed to have a higher plan. They believe it worked out just the way God intended.

I call that the "Lazarus Principle." Remember in Luke 16, how no one could understand why Jesus didn't do the obvious thing when his good friend, Lazarus, was ill? He waited and Lazarus died. The idea is that God had a greater blessing in store for Lazarus and everyone else than that which seemed logical. Instead of healing, there was the miracle of resurrection.

Sometimes sacrificial service turns out that way. Perhaps it could do so more often if we worked more closely with the Miracle Worker himself.

These stories seem to me to say:

1. Sacrificial service to others is impressive.

2. God puts the concern, the love in our hearts and in our minds when we walk with the Lord. Love becomes service to others.

3. God can use anyone, anytime.

4. Parents train, God calls to service.

5. Holding office and performing service aren't the same. Often they go together, but the common denominator is the personal arrangement between God and us humans. Titles are secondary.

6. Service for Christ is based on agape love: love that considers the need, without weighing the outcome, the chances for reward, or the basic worth of the person receiving the service.

These friends wanted you to know:

David Sebastian	Ruth Wolfe Vanosdol
Oscar Seidel	Steve and Cindy Shoop
Ross Minkler	David and Donna Miller
Lorraine Chorlton	Floyd and Marianne Strickland
H. Grant Bentley	Keith O'Neill
Paul Bentley	

A word worth remembering:

"The Christian ideal has not been tried and found wanting. It has been found difficult and left untried."

—G. K. Chesterton[9]

"The religious training of their children was extremely important to our foremothers and forefathers. They just happened to think that home was the best setting for that instruction."
—Merle Strege[10]

"Be examples of the good life ... home lovers ... a good advertisement for the Christian faith."
—Titus 2:5, J. B. Phillips

6

THE BACKBONE: THE HOME

What's the heart of a good home? In today's world, very few families are what has been called "traditional": mom, dad, a couple of children, living together in a home, with mom looking after the children while dad works.

Funny, but as I poke around, looking for what the Church of God means to people, I find few "traditional" homes in yesteryear.

Joe Minkler, for instance, was born and lived for five years on the far western Missouri campgrounds at Carthage. He grew up there getting used to people coming to the campgrounds for various gatherings and bringing their cows with them. "And when we moved to town and returned to the campground for services, we took our cow with us, too," Joe added.

Charles Ludwig spent much of his life in Africa, watching his dedicated, industrious parents work night and day to minister to their neighbors, especially the families of the girls at the Bunyore Girls School.

But Charles says, "My mother told me that before I was born, when she first felt me inside her, she began praying that I would carry the gospel message when I grew up."

How well I recall those depression days in my own home when mom toiled long hours in a public market selling pickles and sauerkraut. In that congested, dirty, godless city there was precious little that would reflect the ideal American way of life.

What I'm trying to say is that for me the Church of God and its people were a special family to our family in those years.

To quote others who seem to look back and see this, too: "The church and the home are special. In fact, one of my earliest memories is that of the church asking our family to host cottage prayer meetings," recalled Jack Hobson. "Out of these came the Woodstock Church of God in Portland, Oregon."

Don Johnson tells of a "parade of church leaders passing through my parents' home when I was young." Bernice Pergrem Salisbury comments: "During the depression years our family with its six children had the privilege of a Christian inheritance because of the Church of God and because my mother, Millie Roberson Pergrem, 'saw the light' in Church of God services in Kentucky in the 1920s."

She continues: "Now, wherever I live or wherever I travel, when I attend a Church of God, I feel at home."

A. Lenn Hartwig remembers that as an infant "my bassinet was placed on a back pew of the Church of God sanctuary." The joy of his life today is to realize what the Church of God has done to shape the lives of his family. "I have the smartest grandson you ever saw. He won't let us eat till we each have our hands folded and he gives thanks for the meal."

Our congregation in Baltimore gave my family a home and gave us a family to love that, honestly, was closer than the family nature had given us. As a child, my parents lifted up the church (the Church of God was the only church we knew) and recommended it to me. As the years went by, I tried fellowship with that church and found, once again, that my parents were telling the truth.

Much has been written through the years of the power of a mother's prayer. I remember with a cringe the terrible prayer my mom shared each day as I headed out to school. It ruined a lot of potential mischief for me. She prayed, "Let Danny be the boy his mother thinks he is."

Pastor Don Smith of Morgantown, North Carolina, remembers a remarkable "coincidence" in the lives of his dad and uncle. "For thirty years my grandmother prayed for her boys. One night my dad was in the woods hunting with a pack of coon dogs. Just like in a story, he heard the singing of a little church that was holding a revival. He tied the dogs and slipped inside. Before the night was over he'd given his heart to Christ.

"But the strange thing was that when he called his brother Lyle in Zanesville, his brother said, 'I'm happy for you Dale. But you be happy with me, too. Last week I gave my life to Christ.' "

And, you know, this "our family/church family" business is a two-way street. Our house was in a second-generation neighborhood in Highlandtown, Baltimore. It would have been easy to give in to the pressures of the mess around us. But mom and dad kept close to the Lord and allowed the Church of God to be their support team.

The Jesse Egly family has been a force in Christian home standards for years. In Danville, Illinois, some old-timers still remember papa and mama Egly bringing the whole family (six children) to church every Sunday, well-behaved, growing, learning, and—as the children remember with a frown—"always on time."

The strengths of the church, carried home each week, have often been guideposts in child-rearing. "From my earliest recollection my mother impressed upon me the three most important choices in life," Paul Tanner relates. "First in priority was conversion. Put God first. Next, marriage: choose carefully the life mate. It's for life. Don't blow it. Third, vocation. Mom would say, 'If God calls you to the ministry, don't stoop to be president.' "

"My mother, Mrs. Edna Stevens, spent time in prayer and Bible study," Arlene Hall remembers. "I'll always be grateful that she helped me make the Bible my own book, to learn to use and enjoy it."

Phyllis Dobson remembers when she was a child and saw Lottie Franklin's picture in the *Gospel Trumpet*. Lottie was reading from *Egermeier's Bible Story Book*. That book has been a Church of God standard for many years, and no Church of God home seemed complete without it.

Lottie's father, Pastor Benjamin J. Franklin, was a gentle, caring man. Lottie later told Mrs. Dobson, "My father preached with all his heart. He preached in love, but presented the truth in a demanding, often stern, manner. He said he preached as though one of his own beloved family members was in the audience and was an unbeliever."

One of the exciting trends in today's church circles is the renewed reinforcement of the ties between church and home. Home Bible studies, neighborhood coffee times, and actual congregations made up of many home churches have become popular again. To me, the hope of the future for the homes of our country lies in the church's strength getting behind the concept of Christian homes. One of the heartbreaking patterns many of us have seen is that of putting the family first, ahead of Christ. Unless the home has something divine to look to, hard times may crush that home. God stands behind a strong union of home and church.

The Christian home begins with the individual convictions of the man and woman who establish that home. The church can't build a home for us. Love for each other isn't enough to have a solid marriage or a good home. Individual dedication to Christ and united submission to God's will must come first.

What does *home* mean to you? For some it means finding a comfortable, familiar worship place when you are far, far from home.

Anne was born and reared in an Anglican church in Sri Lanka, a home led by an Anglican lay preacher: everything in life began and ended with the church.

Rushing out of Sri Lanka with her family, Anne landed in Singapore and, after a year, settled in Canada. Funny an Anglican church could not be found. Anne ended up at the Fairview Church of God: change, shock, deep differences confronted her.

"The meaningful worship, the friendliness of the members, the graciousness of the pastor, the marvelous singing, the inspiring messages—why, even the worship folder was done with so much love that my heart was touched."

She visited, she returned, she stayed. "The church building does not constitute the church," she says. "Nor do rituals, formalities, and the rest. The presence of God does it and God's life in our daily lives: that's the church."

Anne admits to eighty-one years and says in the Church of God she has truly found a home. "This place and these people are what Christ meant when he said, 'I will build my church.'"

One of the funniest and most profound stories I've ever heard came from my own parents' mouths. They met while working on a variety of programs in the local Church of God. He was a confirmed bachelor of forty-plus and she an "unclaimed jewel" herself, well past thirty. But they fell in love.

What they did about it is the interesting part. They agreed to pray about their future. Dad, obviously impatient to get some word, finally blurted out, "Bobbie, God has shown me that I should marry you."

Without batting an eye, she popped out with, "As soon as God talks to me about it, we'll get together."

She says that it seemed forever before they got together, and every time dad came near her he was asking, "Got anything from the Lord yet?" Finally, she tells, one night very late as she lay awake in bed, a light came into the room. She looked up and at the foot of her bed was an oval spot of light on the footboard. My dad's face was framed in that light. An audible voice said, "Marry this Christian worker." She did.

And here I am.

But God came first. God's will came first. No wonder in our home the same standard existed. No wonder the church was our second home.

It is not by accident that God uses family terms. God is father. We are children of God. The church is our mother. Other Christians are sisters and brothers in Christ. To become a Christian is to be born again. We are nurtured and fed and clothed in the Spirit just as a family cares for the well-being of its human members.

The church and the family are so closely knit together that when one suffers, the other suffers, too, and as we build each in solid, God-dictated terms, the other is built as well.

The Church of God ideal is to be in truth the family of God in each community where congregations exist. The ideal is to build the local congregation out of God-filled homes in that community. I like that kind of dream. I like that kind of church.

God's smallest group is found in the home:

1. God works in homes that will admit him, beginning with where that home is in its spiritual life.

2. As with the church, the building or the physical possessions do not identify a good home; the people do. Their spiritual quality determines the fate of the home.

3. God molds moms and dads; moms and dads mold children.

4. Families can accomplish anything families decide to do.

5. God wants to and will actively participate in every area of home life once we invite him to do so.

6. Sometimes the church family becomes more precious than our earthly family.

These friends shared their feelings just for you:

Joe Minkler	Arlene Hall
Merle Strege	Lottie Franklin
Donald J. Smith	Benjamin J. Franklin
Paul Tanner	Jack Hobson
Phyllis Dobson	Donald Johnson
Edna Stevens	Bernice Pergren Salisbury
Charles Ludwig	Millie Roberson Pergren
A. Lenn Hartwig	Anne Canaga Retnam
Jesse and Ida Egly	

A parting word from a wise heart:

"True religion will always produce a clean life, an honest life in the home, community, and world at large."

—H. M. Riggle[11]

"Our churches need help. I see our greatest goal at Warner Press as being a servant to our churches."
—Sara Lindemuth[12]

7

"As God's fellow workers we urge you."
—2 Corinthians 6:1, NIV

SHOULDER TO SHOULDER MINISTRY

Ever heard of *The Gospel Trumpet?*

Today the magazine is called *Vital Christianity,* but back in the early 1900s both the parent company, a publishing plant of the Church of God, and the weekly magazine were called *The Gospel Trumpet.*

In 1903 a small family in Pennsylvania was asked to attend a home prayer meeting. An itinerant evangelist, Anna Martin, led them and passed out copies of the *Gospel Trumpet* and other literature produced by the Church of God.

"My parents became interested," writes Gertrude Helms Heinrichs. As time went by, dozens of personal study times with Anna Martin evolved. She became close to the family. "In fact, she was a professional midwife and delivered my brother Martin," Mrs. Heinrichs remembers.

Rolla Swisher says, "The first broadcast had me." He is referring to the Christian Brotherhood Hour, the official radio program of the Church of God, heard all around the world each week.

"The stimulating choral music, the magnetic, warm voice of Dr. Dale Oldham and the down-to-earth sermon made me a regular listener. When I asked for a printed copy of a sermon, they sent me a copy of the *Gospel Trumpet* containing the sermon. After that, I was a regular subscriber."

The official institutions, groups, ministries, and cooperative projects of the Church of God are truly remarkable. With the freedom evident among us, the programs of these groups are always interesting; but if you ask people in a Church of God congregation, "What brought you to the Church of God?" you'll be amazed at how many heard the radio broadcast, read a *Trumpet*, or attended some conference of the Church of God.

Carl Erskine, Baseball Hall of Fame hero, came to know the Church of God during his early years, living in Anderson, Indiana. He attended Anderson College (now Anderson University) and eventually came back there after his phenomenal baseball career with the Dodgers.

He has this to say about his association with the college: "I am impressed with the life-style that Anderson University develops in its students: the students leave to go around the world, filled with a true spirit and attitude of Christian service."

Probably each college and Bible school has dozens of former students who will claim—as I do—that their alma mater was a crucial influence in shaping their lives. In an age when individualism seems to be reaching its height, the Church of God reaffirms its belief that there are many, many tasks that Christians can best do by cooperating.

It was at a Church of God college that I proposed to my wife of thirty-six years. Without any attempt to parade piety, I say simply that among her virtues was the fact that she was a girl I could pray with comfortably, as well as hold hands with and look at the moon. One of the most satisfying feelings a husband can have is to hear his mother-in-law say she was glad she sent her daughter off to a Church of God college where she met her future husband.

Zena Church (that wonderful mother-in-law) adds another bit of thanksgiving in another field: "One other thing I will always be grateful for in the Church of God is the traveling Lab Schools that our national Board of Christian Education used to sponsor. Teacher training sessions as well as correspondence classes to expand our resources mean a lot. Adam Miller, Don Courtney, Ken Hall, Roscoe Snowden, and George Kufeldt taught me much."

Most of us feel a bit uncomfortable trusting our thinking, our program for life to strangers. Church of God colleges bask in the warmth of personal attention to students' needs. Our publishing house, Warner Press, rejoices at the people who call in on their toll-free number for special attention to orders.

"The Church of God means to me a trust in a group of people," writes Marion Torstenbo. "We sent our daughter off to Anderson University knowing we could feel comfortable that she would be surrounded by loving, Christian people, both at the university and in the Church of God of her choice."

No guarantee that everyone will feel that way, but there's something reassuring about the family feeling I find in the institution of the Church of God. People are people, both in official positions and as recipients of the ministries of the institutions. There are problems and friction and poor communication sometimes, but try to match the batting average you find in the church with that of comparable groups outside the church.

The Gospel Trumpet home was a special place. It was the practical setting for the workers in the Trumpet company. Communal living and cooperative sharing were featured. Located in Anderson, Indiana, near the turn of the century, the focal point was work at the Gospel Trumpet Company, but the "family," the workers, lived together.

"I heard dad tell about butchering hogs and cattle to get fresh meat to the Gospel Trumpet home," recalls Opal Hull Lehnus. "We lived on a farm near Anderson and 'church' was some place we wanted to go to. In fact, I was named Opal after a missionary to West Indies, Opal Brookover."

One of our pioneer leaders, E. E. Byrum, was noted far and wide long before the modern-day faith healers came into the spotlight. His "anointed handkerchiefs" went all across the country, and hundreds of testimonies of healing came pouring into his office. In fact, they say there was a room kept especially to house the discarded braces, crutches, and other helps people had used before God healed them.

"In the summer of 1916, word spread around our community of a tent meeting where people were like gods and had the power to heal people. Many of us went to listen," says Rush S. Thomas. He was impressed. "I told my parents and they attended with me. Then, to our surprise, someone sent us a subscription to the *Gospel Trumpet*. How that changed our lives. I never found out who did it."

Joan Soldano thought she'd discovered heaven when she stumbled onto Pastor Cliff Tierney and the First Church of God in Torrence, California. Her eyes were opened to truth, her heart was touched by the love and concern of the people, and her life was forever changed when she—as an adult—gave her life to Christ.

"When the Lord got hold of me, I gave my all. Then Pastor Tierney asked us all to pitch in and build a church building. I look back in amazement now, but we put our hearts into it and on our own we built a tremendous worship and educational plant that still stands today."

I have to add a personal note about Joan. She always felt attracted to the mission field. Sensing God's call, she prepared herself. She attended a Church of God college, readied herself for the mission field overseas, and waited. She asked, requested, pleaded, and badgered the missions leaders.

No call came. Poor timing was the culprit. For months Joan wondered why God had led her.

Today she can look back and smile. She recalls the time a beautiful new thought came to her. "Why not find a mission field right here at home?"

To cut the story short, Joan and her faithful sidekick, "Bunny" Hobart, have developed the most exciting, most unusual, unique, and intriguing ministry to children you've ever seen. Literally thousands of children in the San Bernardino, California, area know Joanie. She has grandmas whose only ministry is to greet each Sunday school child with a hug; she provides programs for the children of battered women in a local shelter; she supervises round-the-calendar programs for kids in the Church of God (she has workers standing in line, begging to help in the Vacation Bible School each summer).

Well, the "institutional" training Joan had was great. She knows her Christian education principles. But beyond this, God has led Joan Soldano from what she calls "darkness" to a missionary venture among children of all races, all cultures, speaking a wide variety of languages—and all in America. All in a tough, urban, smog-filled, residential mission field called southern California.

The Church of God houses a wide variety of general offices in Anderson, Indiana, as well as a great university and a seminary, the School of Theology. Across the country are state programs and area educational ventures. The colleges draw largely from the area that is geographically near them, but each also appeals to many whose homes are far from the campus.

Each school has its own story. Dr. Barry Callen has produced a landmark for the church, a work that details the historical path each has followed in his great book, *Preparing for Service.*

Around the world are thousands who sing the praises of Azusa University in Azusa, California, of Warner Southern College in Lake Wales, Florida, of Mid-America Bible College in Oklahoma City, Oklahoma, of Warner Pacific College in Portland, Oregon, of Anderson University in Anderson, Indiana, and of Gardner Bible College in Cambrose, Alberta, Canada.

Each program of an agency of the church draws new faces into the Church of God sphere of influence. Reinforcing everything that individuals and congregations do are the powers of our cooperative efforts to share the love and redemption of Jesus Christ.

Maybe it sounds impersonal to you, but the buildings, the classrooms, the publications, and the image of the church as seen in its institutions are attractive to me. They get my attention, and when I investigate and find that the ideas and people behind those programs say something relevant that speaks to me, then I thank God for the "bigness" of the church. The millions raised for missions impress me.

The thousands who read our periodicals find truth there. Even the chance to invest cash in the church's ministries is something special: it says to me that I can earn interest and help those in the church family who can take a loan and make it reach people for Jesus Christ.

A church that can do this means a lot to me.

Experience shows us that

1. Some tasks can be done together that none of us can do alone.

2. The Church of God can be proud of its cooperative ministries.

3. Our institutions and service organizations minister in ways beyond their intention.

4. *Ministry* should have a broad interpretation. If we choose, we can join with God to sanctify vocation, home, and service.

5. Impressive buildings, organization, complex programs, and slick image can never substitute for Christ-filled, dedicated disciples who invest their lives in serving Christ and his church.

6. When Christians put their hearts into their church, nothing is impossible.

These friends contributed to chapter 7:

Gertrude Helms Heinrichs	Anna Martin
Rolla Swisher	Carl Erskine
Marion Torstenbo	Opal Hull Lehnus
Ruth S. Thomas	Joan Soldano
Cliff Tierney	Bunny Hobart
Barry Callen	Zena Church

A parting thought:

Russian giant Alexander Solzhenitsyn had a word to say about the coordination that can only come from above.

> I look back in wonder at the path which I alone could never have found, a wondrous path through despair to this point from which I, too, could transmit a reflection of your rays. As much as I still reflect, you will give me; but as much as I cannot take up, you will have already assigned to others.[13]

You are a creation of God. You were first conceived in the thoughts of the universe's greatest thinker. You are like no one else. You were designed individually, lovingly, and purposefully.
—quoted in Maurice Berquist's *The Miracle and Power of Blessing*, ©Warner Press.[14]

"If anyone is ill, he should send for the Church Elders."
—James 5:13, J. B. Phillips

8

HEALING

"How did I find the Church of God? That's easy. Dr. E. E. Wolfram was preaching about how God could heal sickness, and my wife and I came forward to pray for her healing. God healed her and that got my attention."

Today John Boedeker pastors a new, thriving Church of God congregation in Florida and serves as chairperson of the Publication Board of the Church of God.

Such a story, simple and understandable, has been repeated around the world for over one hundred years. Hope for the sick, a breath of encouragement for those who felt medicine had let them down: these take note when the Church of God says, "You can be healed."

Can you hear the heartfelt cry of joy in these words? "When my daughter Linda was four, her blood would not clot. For over eighteen months we made trips to doctors, hospitals, and specialists. We went to the famed Bowman Clinic in Johnson City, Tennessee, after she almost bled to death at home.

"Then a Church of God pastor anointed her and prayed for her. I was sick myself, sick from worry. The Lord wonderfully healed my daughter and he healed me, too. I even went on to help in that summer's Vacation Bible School at the Church of God." Grace W. Flanary lives in Norton, Virginia, and no matter what you may say about her testimony, she gives God the glory. Can you imagine her being neutral in her attitude toward the Church of God?

Much has been said through the years about the healing ministry of E. E. Byrum. "But folks ought to know about his wife," writes Phyllis Dobson. "While he was ministering around the country, she was quietly ministering in another way. She was a caring woman who saw beyond the physical need of the body to the home situations where illness had struck. She always had a basket of food for the homes her husband visited. In her own home was a worn out cookstove, and she wore the same old coat for many years, all to save money so she could help those in need."

One of the cornerstones of divine healing in the Church of God tradition has always been the vital need for faith by the person who is ill. If at all possible, the spiritual condition of the sick person needs ministering first.

"Do you believe Jesus can heal you?" was the question asked of Frances Benfield when the pastor came to see her. Only a tot, Frances said with all her heart, "I do."

Then, instead of praying immediately for Frances, the pastor did an odd thing. "Frances, tonight in church at eight o'clock sharp the entire congregation is going to be praying for you. At that time you put your hand in your mother's hand and pray with us. Will you do it?" Frances agreed.

She recalls, "I remember that I kept asking my mother what time it was. At eight, we prayed, and God healed me right then." It was as simple as that.

I like a church that does the right things and does them in a simple, straightforward way.

A great host of people loved and respected Paul Clausen. But he was afflicted with a debilitating illness, Huntington's disease. His wife Barbara worked with him faithfully to the end, some twenty years after this beautiful pastor/singer was struck down.

At his funeral Paul's friends gathered to renew their faith in God's love and care. But Barb phrased it best. In a letter she wrote to Paul, she closed with these words: "Through the silence of a million hours our hands clasped, our eyes have said so much. And as you go into that bright tomorrow where pain is gone, where sorrow is no more, rejoice in him whose grace was all sufficient, and wait for me upon that golden shore."

The Church of God believes in divine healing, but a higher belief is in God's eternal plan for those who follow him. Some move into that eternal life from a bed of pain. Our faith copes with this when we really know our God. Be sure to read Paula Oldham Johnson's touching story in chapter 11.

"Any old church was okay for us as we moved around." Ernest Sparks remembers that his mom died when he was eight and his lumberjack dad moved from camp to camp. "I didn't believe in Santa Claus or the Easter Bunny, and I certainly didn't believe that stuff about Jesus Christ," Ernest said.

By 1942 he had been drafted into the army, where, as he says, "I had been trying to be an atheist." Upon graduating from an army surgical technician school, Ernest began to think. "The human body is too complicated and too well organized to have gotten there without a Master Mind creating it." He was thinking, but he felt confused. "Why had a God put me in a world and abandoned me?" Admitting that it was oddball thinking, Ernest says, "I felt God owed it to me to make an appearance and introduce himself to me."

A man visited Ernest. "He said he had felt led by God to tell me that there was a meeting to take place that I should attend. I went. Ruby Kitchen was speaking."

Ernest gave his heart to Christ; but the start of his discovery of truth was a confrontation with the details of the human body and the necessity Ernest felt for a Creator. That is at the root of all doctrines of divine healing. The Creator can fix the creation. I understand that kind of logic.

"Healing" sometimes means help beyond the ills of the body: mental health, emotional healing, families being mended of sad, divisive forces.

Hillery Rice has been an outstanding pastor in the Church of God for more than fifty years. He has had a happy, spiritually blessed marriage. "But not always," he says. "At one point in our marriage, God saved our family. We were pulling apart, but the church saved us."

He looks back on his childhood and remembers the challenging example his family provided. "Mom was the strength. Her favorite doctrine was divine healing. We never went to the doctor.

"Mom must have been the original positive thinker. She always had a good word to say to and about everyone, without exception. One well-meaning saint asked her, 'Can you say a good word about the devil?' "

"She thought for a moment and quietly said, 'Well, he is a hard worker.' "

Mom Rice found the Church of God and Hillery remembers a great sigh coming from her. "I knew God had a church somewhere like this," she said. "Now I've found it."

From this home three Church of God ministers have come: Hillery, Herschell, and Eugene.

That connection between the faith of the one who is sick and the healing of the body probably comes from James' words: "The prayer of faith shall save the sick . . . and if he have committed sins, they shall be forgiven him" (5:15).

Mary H. Morgan's mother was ill for a long time.

"When mom was well, she went to the Church of God. In those days there weren't many doctors, but the medicine man would come by once or twice a year and mom would stock up. The mantel over the fireplace had all kinds of medicine.

"When mom got saved, she threw away all the medicine. We believed in divine healing. For myself, I was only too happy to see the castor oil and Black Draught go. They used to be given for just about any sickness."

The family grew spiritually. Mary married a pastor. "I remember the Church of God people praying for us," she said. "The church guided my life. I thank the Lord for the Church of God."

No wonder.

The term "divine healing" has taken a beating through the years. But, friend, be careful: just because there are frauds and false teachers doesn't mean there isn't the real thing.

For many of us, healing includes all that can be done humanly and all that God does, regardless of where or when.

"I was told I needed a heart transplant," Rory Romaine tells us. "As the transplant team went to work, so did the church. My wife appealed and all across the country the people of God were praying. I went into surgery with the confidence that the outcome was in the hands of God. I was secure. This was something that I had developed from a life spent in the Church of God; it wasn't some strong faith mustered for this crisis occasion."

Rory is back to pastoring and still in love with God's church.

I can't vouch for it, but E. I. Carver vividly

remembers the time his grandfather had his right arm pulled completely from its socket. The doctors went to work, but didn't set it properly. They wanted to break the arm again and reset the affected area. Grandpa said no!

Carver's mother began to pray. "Fasting and prayer followed and God miraculously reset the arm."

"Shattered glass hit my mother as the car rolled and rolled, ending up on its top," Herb Ortman shares. "Everyone was okay except mom and after we pulled her out, the flow of blood was frightening."

Some Church of God people helped, and the blood stopped. "But what I remember is the prayer time at home after we got mom safely in bed. We little children bowed by our chairs. If ever the listening ear of God has been open to the earnest pleas of needy children, it was that night. Our childish voices expressed our desperate plight. Mom needed a touch."

Herb's mother recovered and he remembers the deep scars she carried for the rest of her life. "More than the scars was the family experience. One little boy carried that prayer meeting with him down through life. That prayer meeting and the saints of the Church of God have entrenched faith into my character forever," explains Herb.

If you ask around, you can probably find a

dozen examples of God's healing touch on people right in the Church of God near you. Little media attention is given to these week in, week out healings, but they're real.

What happens in the hearts and spirits of the people involved is real, too. Our conviction is that this is the vital part: the body ends in the grave, but the spirit lives forever. Better a sick body and a well soul than the opposite.

Our God is a personal, caring God:

1. God cares enough to heal us when we extend our faith and fit into God's plans.

2. God usually involves Christians in the healing process.

3. Caring for people—sharing in the healing ministry—hasn't been an attention-getting facet of Church of God life. It's natural, a vital part of everyday living.

4. Christians often hold on to Christ in faith and endure great pain and suffering, and they never know why.

5. We have had the good sense to realize that God uses human medical knowledge as part of his healing ministry.

6. The faith we need when we are ill should be an extension of the faith we have been developing in other areas of our lives.

7. Teaching our children God's love in healing is an investment that pays off in lifelong benefits.

These friends and their testimonies are included in this chapter on healing:

Paul and Barbara Clausen	Maurice Berquist
Frances Benfield	John Boedeker
E. E. Wolfram	Grace W. Flanary
Phyllis Dobson	Ernest Sparks
Mary H. Morgan	Rory Romaine
E. I. Carver	Herb Ortman
Hillery Rice	E. E. and Mrs. Byrum

One last word of testimony:

"The doctors talked to me straight. Cancer. Surgery was necessary. I told them how God had touched me, but they set the date anyhow. When they did surgery, they were puzzled because they found nothing. I told them it was because God touched me."

—Frances Benfield[15]

Sunday is worship time. And testimony time. God works in all of this. No play at religion but real dedication to the Lord and His service.
—Jack Hobson[16]

"Be strong and steady, always abounding in the Lord's work, for you know that nothing you do for the Lord is ever wasted."
—1 Corinthians 15:58, Living Bible

9

OPPORTUNITY

Throngs of people in this country seem to be shouting, "Please give me something to do about what I believe, about what I feel, and about the things that ought to be done."

The church means opportunity to me, a chance to become involved in something that matters. From the things I've been hearing from others in the Church of God, this is something precious to them, too.

Stories about Ross Minkler are legendary in the Church of God. Most of the old-timers can recall a tent meeting, a song service, a camp meeting, or revival when Ross was part of a tremendous experience of joy and victory and salvation. His touch meant a great deal to many people across the country and across the years.

Inez Cobb recalls Ross's ministry in the oasis of Skull Valley, Arizona, back in the 1920s. "We met in a school house that had been used for dances on Saturday night; one of our joys was seeking out the places where dancers had hidden their whiskey bottles. We'd empty them and refill them with vinegar.

"Usually the Sunday morning services were Brother Ross's single preaching time. But one time we had a revival, and sure enough, on Saturday night a gang of drunken cowboys on their horses came by looking for the usual Saturday night dance.

"When they saw that a revival was in progress, they were angry and started shooting off their guns. Some of the shots came into the school house. Quick as a flash the men in the congregation raced out, pulled the men from their horses, and forced them to sit through the revival service on the front row. They were pretty peaceful by the end of the service."

Minkler and hundreds of other traveling preachers were often ill-trained for ministry, but the church gave them the opportunity to respond to God's call and serve, and God trained them.

In today's church the ministers are better trained, more aware of needs and opportunities for service. With the advance in education and sophistication in our society, much more is demanded of their ministry.

Out in Wichita, Kansas, Pastor Ray Cotton has done a remarkable job of putting together a team of leaders, of cooperating with God's boundless source of ideas, and of opening the doors of opportunity to all who want to do something about what they feel and believe.

"If we are successful, it is due in large measure to our attitude of openness: I feel it's the spirit of the Church of God, of practicing a unity of spirit that welcomes everyone who has a desire to be part of us and find a place of service in the church body." Pastor Cotton continues, "The community has sensed our spirit of openness, and now we are experiencing their openness to the message of the Church of God."

If you are ever out that way, you'll be impressed with the huge corps of volunteer workers who have found satisfying ministry in the program of that church.

As you can imagine, many of those who remember the early days of the Church of God are now well advanced in age; nursing homes and retirement villages all across the land are home to many of these pioneers.

Lois E. McWilliams is one of them. Her

beautiful memories of the church in the days of long ago are filled with people who "heard a call and answered." Her own sister was a persistent and faithful lay leader. Her pastor, C. E. Byers, was a tireless minister. And her own personal work through the years has been one long string of ministries, always seeking new ventures for her Lord.

Hollis Pistole has served the church as pastor, national leader, and teacher of ministerial students in our School of Theology. His start was in a storefront Church of God congregation in Detroit, Michigan. "I was surrounded by a supportive group of Christians who nurtured my fledgling faith. I was impressed by their efforts to be more than " 'mere Christians.' "

Hollis felt his call to the ministry and he says, "I received a positive affirmation from the congregation." I like the four qualities that Hollis says he appreciates about the Church of God:

1. "Theology—we are not locked into a rigid creedal position."

2. "Membership—not joining but seeking to be part of God's family."

3. "Bible—our focus is on the Bible as it points us to Christ."

4. "Fellowship—a joyful bond that unites Church of God believers wherever they are found."

The list goes on. People "seeing" the truth, responding to the message, and wanting to do something about it.

The names are part of Church of God history. "E. E. Byrum," writes his niece, Jessie R. Schieve, "traveled widely. I went with him and the family on a six-months' trip to South America." Jessie knew Byrum, F. G. Smith, and a host of other early Church of God leaders. All put shoe leather to what they believed.

For many who felt the inner drive to serve and minister, the beginning was a revelation of the tremendous needs in the world around them. Jane Bradford reveals: "W. E. Monk and Earl Wells opened my childish eyes to the needy world out there. Our family was poor, but these men stuck images in our minds of the wealth we had in knowing Jesus Christ."

Jane is talented in a wide variety of fields, not the least of which is art. "When I was eleven, the Church of God sponsored an art contest at the Birmingham, Alabama, state campgrounds. I entered and won first place. That seemed to seal my dedication to give whatever talents I had to Jesus.

"Do you know what I remember? One judge saw that on my poster (the one entered in the contest) I had made a smudge and tried to cover it up. Instead of commenting on the smudge, he commended me on the way I'd reworked the mess and made it appealing. That did it. I stood tall for weeks."

The examples set for youngsters in the church continue. Laura Alice Rickert was only thirteen when, over sixty years ago, she was asked to go to meet the train and welcome F. G. Smith to town. "He was coming to hold a revival," she said. This prominent Church of God leader and others like Charles Naylor, the great song writer, impressed, molded, and challenged the lives of many young people like Laura Alice.

Moreover, those who were impressed by our pioneers have themselves become examples to the youngsters of today. In East Tennessee "Sister Simmons" may be a mature, grandmotherly type now, but I vividly recall that as a young woman she excelled in the nursery department. She spent many fruitful, happy years teaching and loving the little ones.

In a memorable meeting of the board of Christian education there was a crisis: "No one will teach the senior high girls." The discussion swirled around and finally silence surrounded us. A meek voice spoke up from the back row.

"May I try teaching them?" Charlotte Simmons spoke up. Her teach them? Why, they would eat her alive. She was too fragile, too quiet and self-sacrificing to handle that gang of girls.

Not having any other option, we "threw her to the female wolves." In the months that followed a transformation took place. Not only didn't the group demolish the "fragile" teacher, they sat quietly as she taught in her quiet way week after week.

The group grew until they burst out of the classroom and met for years in the last two (then three, then four) rows of the sanctuary.

The side benefits grew, too. Charlotte blossomed. The girls came for counseling so much that the teacher sometimes had to make appointments. They found their ideal teacher and she found a brand-new ministry. The opportunity arose and God helped the church fill it.

You really ought to read the whole manuscript by Nyle Kardatzke, "The Clock of the Covenant." To summarize, Nyle recalls that when he was three years of age, a big wall clock at the rear of the sanctuary caught his attention.

One day, as Nyle gazed at the clock, he thought he heard the pastor say of Moses, "God ordered that the tablets be placed in the clock (ark) of the Covenant." From then on, the clock was the Clock of the Covenant to him.

Because, in his childish mind, God's laws were in that wall clock, Nyle took the teachings of the church seriously. Lots of humorous things are attached to the experiences he recalls, but one important fact rises above the others.

The old clock made the people, the events, the services, and the ministries of the Church of God of supreme importance to him. The church family was a fellowship in which to share the most important experiences of life, an opportunity to be part of something vital.

Aged people have always touched my heart. As I get nearer their age, I appreciate the values of experience, wisdom, and caution. But the quality that surprised me most in growing up was the sharp edge of adventure, the take-a-chance-for-the—Lord attitude that so many of these veterans had.

Many a time I've seen these grey-haired warriors pitch in to help a dangerously drunk tough guy on the street or "cold turkey" knock on doors, street after street, in behalf of the church.

In his later years my own dad found a most satisfying and appropriate ministry in being a "pastor's pastor" to several of our congregation's ministerial leaders.

In his later years Brother Kroh sat in church services and designed the interior woodwork for the remodeling of the sanctuary. How well I remember sitting near him and staring with wide eyes at the complex sketches, dimensions, and descriptions of the hand-tooled woodwork.

Then the day came for the first service in the newly transformed sanctuary. It was all so new, so beautiful; but, of course, my eyes went right to the harmony, the complicated details, and the sheer majesty of the woodwork. In all his woodworking career, Brother Kroh never produced anything so marvelous as that chancel in Baltimore. God gave him the opportunity to use his talents and this solid old saint of the church came through. (See Exodus 31 for the way God called special workers in metal to help on the tabernacle.)

In our day the parade of people in the Church of God who see a need, an opportunity, and respond continues sometimes in odd and unusual ways.

Walter Toner once told his pastor, "Out in front of our house is a main thoroughfare with thousands of cars going by each day. In the middle is a grassy median strip. How about if I dress up in a clown suit, sit in a rocking chair, and advertise the car wash on the church parking lot?" Though an unused suggestion, it surely would have gotten attention.

Bessie Blankenship exudes talent. One of the oddest is an exceptional skill in rubbing and massaging feet. Sounds like a truly weird talent, but all over southern California are people who always call Bessie when they have foot trouble. She says God gave her the gift.

Perhaps the most astounding example of the opportunities that Church of God people have responded to is the ongoing effort that Tina Houser shows in finding ministries and getting them into action. As a pastor's wife, she has skills that won't quit. When the salary was low, she discovered that the small town she was in had no "Welcome Wagon" program, so she organized one, helped it grow, and sold it.

In that same town she learned of a number of professional people who needed official papers, documents, and records typed and reproduced in a high quality manner. She formed a typing service and had more work than she could do.

One Christmas she formed a service of making hand-dipped chocolates. It was a real winner as people from all walks of life bought up the delicious specialties as quickly as Tina could make them.

Unusual? Yes, and even more so when you consider that from high school days this campus queen has had a painful and crippling form of arthritis. She spends a good deal of her life either in bed or in an electric wheelchair. Nevertheless she is happy, fulfilled, loved, and appreciated. She's discovered the joy of finding a need and filling it.

I like people like Tina.

I like a church that produces that kind of woman.

Maybe these ideas sum it all up:

1. The church in action is our chance to do something about what we say we believe.

2. As with the founding of our nation, many people sacrificed to make today's church as ready as it is to spread the gospel; opportunity often means hard work without harvest.

3. Presenting the gospel to the community openly communicates a freedom and opportunity that is easily understood.

4. The freedom prized by people in the Church of God affords a beautiful variety of opportunities for service and developing of skills.

5. Through the years, the needs and chances to meet them took precedence over committees, boards, and bylaws. "Hang loose and get the job done" is not a new slogan.

6. Children are impressionable: they should have chances to live their faith without waiting till they "grow up."

7. When people have confidence in people, no request is too extreme.

These friends shared their lives in chapter 9:

Jessie R. Schieve	Tina Houser
Jack Hobson	Inez Cobb
Bessie Blankenship	Ray Cotton
Jane Bradford	Ross Minkler
Charlotte Simmons	Lois E. McWilliams
Hollis Pistole	Laura Alice Rickert
Nyle Kardatzke	"Brother Kroh"
Walter Toner	

A reminder to think about:

"If we live at the same level of affluence as other people who have our level of income, we are probably giving away too little. Obstacles to charity include greed for luxurious living, greed for money itself, fear of financial insecurity and showing pride."

—Kathryn Aun Lindskoog[17]

"God will do his own communicating if we can but help create learning and experiencing situations where there is openness to his own ways of making himself known."
—Harold L. Phillips[18]

TRUTH, BIBLE TRUTH

Doctrine can come from many sources: church conferences; strong, charismatic leaders. Heritage and the culture itself can provide teachings that men and women will fight and die for.

One reason the Church of God means a lot to me is that from the earliest days the only authoritative source for doctrine has been the Bible.

Yes, there were strong leaders who for a time influenced the doctrines and practices of the Church of God. In time, however, the church regained its perspective and fell back again on the traditional question, "What does the Bible say about it?"

Yes, I know about some of the practices and customs that arose with no explanation other than prejudice and habit. But one truly remarkable fact emerges: in time, the balance is regained and the words and intent of the Bible hold sway.

Kathleen Buehler tells about her grandfather, Daniel Gerald Davey: British by birth, a resident of the United States, a volunteer in the U.S. Army in France in World War I. Daniel read his Bible. He "had a vision of the church. He was not a Christian, though he had enjoyed being around church activities and church people throughout his life. He 'saw the church' in his mind and heart."

In time as he kept seeking, he attended a service at the North Cove Boulevard Church of God in Toledo, Ohio. He heard the preacher explain the church from the Bible and the interpretation fit exactly with the concept he had found in the trenches of WW I. He leaned over to his wife. "This is it. This is truth." Sixty years of service to Christ followed. God, the Bible, and the church had come together.

The dirty, crowded neighborhood in which I was reared in Baltimore included an equal number of whiskey bars and churches. Methodist, Presbyterian, several Roman Catholic parishes, and a sprinkling of ethnic congregations proclaimed a wide variety of doctrinal positions each week. The kids among whom I played and studied held some odd and peculiar views on religious matters. Mostly they had a poor opinion of the church.

To this day, the amazing thing about that neighborhood was the continual stream of people who sought out my Church of God parents and asked advice and counsel from them. The only answer I have for this phenomenon is that their wisdom was based solely on what they found in the Bible and their own personal lives were spotless. They believed the Bible and lived it.

Richard Wagner of New Castle, Indiana, can fill in the denominational names, but his report is echoed all across the country. "When I had a question, it was answered from the Bible. When I had a need, someone responded to help me. Even now, they take me to the grocery store anytime I call them," he says. He calls the church the "reformation movement," an early designation for the Church of God.

A woman preacher leading services in a pool hall? "Yes, and the pool hall was painted red, too," remembers Mary Lile of Louisville. "They came to scoff, but even though I was only seven, I remember being impressed that there was something different about the way Emma Meyer explained the Bible."

In the years that have followed that doctrinal/Bible emphasis in the beginning, many church leaders have come to the fore with impressive credentials in Bible scholarship. Some were seminary trained, others self-trained, and many seemed to have been given a special gift from God for the ministry of understanding the Bible and applying it to everyday living.

"I never saw or heard another person who knew the Bible like F. G. Smith," Naomi Melton of Rickman, Kentucky, remembers. Her praise of an early Church of God leader can be echoed with different names, depending on what part of the world you check.

All the stories of what the Bible meant to Church of God people are not stories covered with sentiment and dust. Even today, people hear the froth and sugary sweetness of a gospel with no ethical or moral requirements and seek for truth. Others are bound by some dictatorial cult-styled leader and seek for release, for freedom, for the real thing.

Linda McCormack speaks with some hesitancy: "I had known these people all my life (forty-three years) and many of my relatives still belong to the group." She's speaking of an ultrafundamentalist group in Minnesota, a group with no official name, no records, no pastors, and no offerings.

It sounds very "biblical," doesn't it? Yet, while these people (probably numbering less that 100,000 around the world) seek a faith that is absolutely rooted in the Bible, Linda saw things differently. "After searching the scriptures and praying, God revealed to me that they were wrong and that I should get out.

"It was hard. But I had a 'born again' experience and broke away. I began to look elsewhere. After searching across the country, I found what I was looking for in a Church of God congregation in Clovis, New Mexico. I found it, and I still wonder at how God led me to this truth after all those years in that group in Minnesota."

What she's saying is the other side of our stand on Bible truth. No rules forged by human minds or special interpretations outside the Bible: but also an openness to Bible truth so that if anyone disagrees with the church there is still a place for her or him. The Bible is so vast, with such far-reaching dimensions, covering so great a span of history that the considerations we must take in interpreting it are endless. It is unthinkable to Church of God people to have one specific interpretation of each point of truth in the Bible.

Washing dishes isn't exciting to most young girls. Phyllis was no exception. Yet, evening after evening she toiled at the sink with her sister as the after-dinner chores were completed.

Dad did his part. What a part! He would sit by the window, read his Bible out loud and comment. "O, the endless hours it seemed for us to hear the Bible while we were at the dishes," said Phyllis.

You see, Phyllis's dad, Homer Gillespie, had "found" the Church of God in that classic way, often repeated down through the years. Charles Bolen visited Homer and they "talked Bible." When Charley went home, he sent a year's subscription to *The Gospel Trumpet* to the Gillespie home.

"Why, this is what I believe," Homer blurted out after reading the first issue.

So, like it or not, the Gillespie girls got a double dose of what was good for them each evening as dad lectured and the dishes sparkled. But it worked. It carved and molded and had its effect on Phyllis. She is married to Phil Kinley. They are lifelong missionaries to Japan.

"My early Bible teaching has been something special. My parents and the Church of God taught me, and this has guided me all through my life," proclaims Floyd Sellers. He and a host of others can testify to the value of early training. In the Church of God, that has meant Bible training.

Looking back, many of us see the shaping that took place in our lives because of the Bible. "It's full of good promises that we need to remember," is the way Fay Frame puts it. As she nears the one-hundred-year mark, Fay can look back on parents taught by D. S. Warner and on a life of service in the churches of the San Joaquin Valley of California. She trusts a church whose teachings are founded on the Bible.

If we follow the Bible faithfully, will all things work out just fine? Well, maybe. But sometimes it doesn't seem as if they do.

Charley Lee is a plumber, a Christian who has a plumbing business. Charley works hard. He's good at his job. In the course of his company's growth, Charley trusted some people in the office he should not have trusted. As time went by the Internal Revenue Service caught Charley's company at fault for failing to report a sizable chunk of income.

Charley was arrested, brought into federal court, and sent to prison. He served a week or two and was released. "I just wanted him to hear those steel doors clang shut," the judge said. "He's a good man, but he is responsible for his company."

The day before he was to be taken to prison Charley said something we all needed to hear. "Tomorrow they take me to prison. Pray for me, but please don't feel sorry for me. The way I've got it figured out is this: I want to go to heaven and the road to heaven runs right through this prison. I go to prison, on the way to heaven. That's the only path for me to take—through prison to heaven. Now, I'd be a fool to try to go some other way, wouldn't I?" Charley's a bigger, better man for the experience. He stood true and it wasn't easy.

The Bible is not a songbook, but, my, how many wonderful, singable songs have been created based on its contents.

Many church people recall the great quartet song of a few years back, "Ezekiel Saw the Wheel." The Christian Brothers quartet was singing it for Fred Waring and the Pennsylvanians, auditioning for a special program the great conductor was planning.

Fred was impressed. He called to his staff and the great corps of singers in the studio. "Hey, gather around and listen to these boys."

They gathered. The quartet sang, "I Bowed on My Knees and Cried Holy." It was moving. In a church setting there would have been shouts of praise and amens. But in that cold, commercial studio there was silence. No one wanted to breathe when the song ended. Sniffles were heard; tears were wiped. The hard hearts had been softened. Fred cleared his throat and addressed his co-workers.

"Boys and girls, I know why you sing. I pay you. These boys sing because they have something down inside." It was a special moment. I thank God for the Church of God era that included the Christian Brothers quartet.

Jim and Joyce Young have stood true, and it hasn't been easy for them, either. Grape-growers in the bountiful "westlands" around Kerman, California, the Youngs have had to sell off some of their land in recent years to avoid bankruptcy.

But they grew up in the Church of God. The solid Bible teachings told them, "Stand firm and trust God." It is not easy.

The blows that have tested them have not been the failed crops or the rain and wind ruining the raisin crop on the ground.

It is what happened to their boys—two boys, midtwenties, each a promising young adult in the very blossom of life. Each had been raised in that Church of God, Bible-oriented home. Each was killed horribly in auto wrecks just a mile from each other. No reason. No explanation from God. Seemingly, a senseless waste. The community had been twice hit with tragedy, a Church of God congregation twice struck by disaster. A home had been deprived of two stars whose empty Christmas stockings still hang each year over the fireplace.

But the inner strength that comes from God, that comes from an unlimited commitment to Christ, that comes from reading, studying, believing, and living by a Holy Bible: this strength and the love and support of a church family speaks volumes about the Church of God.

I like a church that can do such things to beautiful people.

The thread of the chapter isn't hard to follow:

1. The Bible is central in the doctrines of the Church of God.

2. This was probably more evident in past times than now; maybe we ought to be more obvious today.

3. When truth-seeking people hear truth, something inside clicks.

4. Preaching it and living it are essential to integrity.

5. The modern increase of cults coupled with the fast reporting of the media make for a great many attractive imitations of the truth for us and our children.

6. Learning at an early age impresses deeply: teaching the Bible to our children at an early age is good stewardship.

7. The Bible is true, whether or not our living by it results in joy, satisfaction, and pleasure for us.

8. When we follow God, God will not desert us nor lead us astray.

These friends gave of themselves in this chapter:

Homer and Ruth Gillespie	Emma Meyer
Harold L. Phillips	Linda McCormack
Kathleen Buehler	Floyd Sellers
Mary Lile	Charles Lee
F. G. Smith	Fay Frame
Charles Bolen	Richard Wagner
Jim and Joyce Young	Naomi Melton
Leonard Frame	Phyllis Kinley
Daniel Gerald Davey	

Some landmark quotes to remember:

"As the marsh-hen secretly builds on the watery sod, behold I will build me a nest on the greatness of God."

—Sidney Lanier[19]

"If a man hasn't discovered something that he will die for, he isn't fit to live."

—Martin Luther King, Jr.[20]

"We want to introduce people to life, fresh and new every day."
—Gilbert W. Stafford[21]

"I will live again—and you will too."
—John 14:19, Living Bible

11

LIVING, DYING

The gospel of Jesus Christ is very specific on life and death.

"He who believes in me will live, even though he dies; and whoever lives and believes in me will never die" (John 11:25, NIV).

Anyone who has served the church very long has seen amazing examples of people facing death and smiling, of finding a loved one near death and facing it with a strong heart. Many reading these words have put an extraordinary degree of faith in God at some point when all other helps failed.

An exceptional example of courage, wisdom, and faithfulness to Christ came to me not long ago. Many Church of God people remember Dr. W. Dale Oldham and remember him with joy, respect, and genuine love.

In this chapter I want to turn a few pages over to "Dr. Dale's" granddaughter, Paula Oldham Johnson. She's the daughter of gospel singer Doug Oldham and his wife Laura Lee.

Her insight on life and death touched me. Whether or not you knew her grandfather, I think she has something to say about what the Church of God means to her, and all of us.

This is her story.

Papa, Polly and Me
Paula Oldham Johnson

I grew up listening to my grandfather, Dr. Dale Oldham, preach his powerful sermons on the church from many pulpits across the country. I also heard him struggle with the realities of human behavior around the church and around the dinner table. He had a way of making the pieces fit. They did not clash; they fit together and made sense.

I remember hundreds of days of being with him. My earliest recollections of him are as a powerful preacher in the great Park Place Church of God in Anderson.

I guess I was a little afraid of him when I was young, but when I went to the beautiful house on Seventh Street where he and Polly [Mrs. Oldham] lived, I felt a little more at ease in approaching him. I can see him now, wearing his chef's long, white, starched apron: he fried the keilbasa while Polly cut warm blueberry pie.

As I grew older and matured, I think he mellowed out, too. When John and I had our family, we all loved the precious times at the Oldham house in Anderson. The last summers together were the best: picnics and family dinners topped the list. We secretly called Grandpa "General Patton" as he sent out orders for food and fun and scheduling. Dad [Doug Oldham] would get a call with orders on what should be brought. And how we loved those Fourth of July parades in Anderson.

At Christmas—his last one—the gathering was memorable. He knew he had inoperable cancer. On Christmas Eve, Papa [Dr. Oldham] pulled out a pocket-size book and said he wanted to read a few chapters from one of his favorite books.

As he began to read, we began to laugh. The roar increased and we laughed till we cried. About half way through the book he said he'd finish reading it on Christmas Day. He did. It was a precious moment for the whole family.

On Christmas afternoon, with the ball game on TV, he and I sat together. Suddenly he looked at me and spoke.

"I don't mind leaving, except for Polly. I've always taken care of her and I don't want her to be alone."

All I could manage was an "I know." My emotions were too raw even to be able to speak. But I had to tell him what I felt. I wanted to say, "Don't worry," and "We'll take care of her," or, "I love you" would have helped. I couldn't. But he knew.

A few days later my phone rang. Papa, I thought. But, no, it was my own mother. On a Florida concert tour my dad had collapsed in an airport, and he was in the hospital. They were running tests.

Everyone we knew was praying. No one was much worried; dad had been sick before and always bounced back just fine.

Then mom called again. I sat stunned as she told me of cancer of the colon. The news was grim—immediate surgery, and, worse: no promises. "Just pray" was the plea, and pray we did. All across the country prayer chains went into action. The Church of God rallied in a touching way.

Then another call: Polly called to say Papa had collapsed at home. He was in a med center. She had a room nearby and could walk over to see him anytime.

Every day I could I drove over to see them. Polly was deeply concerned. When I got back home each time, I would call mom and give her the latest.

I have to tell you I had some questions for God during those days. When I called mom, she'd tell me how dad was.

There was the night mom called in tears. Dad had the operation and when mom saw him with all the tubes and wires connected to him, it had hit her hard. The doctors could only tell her that it had been a malignancy and they "hoped" they had gotten it in time.

O how I yearned to be with mom and dad. Yes, I knew I was needed with Papa. One of my questions for God: "Why both of them at the same time?" These two had been our strength, and now both were threatened at once. One was terminal and the other in a desperate fight for life.

But the Lord sustained us, somehow. Each day God gently gave us the strength we needed. I can look back now and thank God for his blessings and kindness.

I remember one afternoon. Polly and I sat by Papa's bedside; he was asleep. She opened her purse and took out a letter, worn and crinkled with age. "He wrote me this back in the '50s. He was on an airplane flying to some meeting."

Not knowing quite what to think, I opened the letter Papa had written to Polly and began to read—no way I can ever forget its impact.

"Some of these times, the road will end for one of us, breaking for a time the romance which still thrills me after being married to you all these years. But we have so lived, and are living, that any such occurrence that men call death can scarcely be looked on as tragedy. Nothing, not even death, can rob us of the riches we have shared.

The interruption will be but for a while and afterward, please God, I shall walk with you, hand in hand, in a valley of flowers and sparkling streams, with a range of towering mountains—snow-capped—along the western horizon.

Let's make a date. We'll rendezvous beside a heavenly mountain stream; we'll dip a cup of cool water; there we can picnic forever and climb the peaks without ever tiring.

Someday perhaps I'll look down, even as I'm now doing from eight-thousand feet, on this earth for the last time. I won't be too sad when that moment comes. But I would like to be able to say, "I have fought a good fight, I have finished my course, I have kept the faith."

You and I don't talk about these things much, my dear, but then you and I know there isn't much need. We each understand.

But don't forget: we have a date. Somewhere over there, where the grass comes right down to the water: you'll know the place when you see it. There will be two white swans swimming slowly close to the shore, and all around them, mirrored in the quiet water, you will see the reflections of those mountains, the fleecy clouds, the perfect sky.

Till then, let's live so close to God that nothing on this earth can jeopardize our life with him and each other."

Dale

Down in Florida the word was exciting: dad amazed the doctors with a miraculous recovery. Too soon for the doctors, he flew home to Ohio, there to be near Papa as his life ebbed away.

When dad arrived, Papa was only semiconscious. Dad stayed by the bedside, reading from the Psalms and singing quietly to Papa as only dad can. Today we say little about those moments he had with Papa, but we're all sure Papa heard and rejoiced. We feel as if his mind traced the trail of his "prodigal" son who came back to Christ, went into the ministry, and now was there to minister to him in his last hours.

When I arrived, Polly was by the bedside. I sat with her. As we sat in silence, we were startled to see Papa open his eyes. It was the first time in many days.

Polly took his hand. Papa said nothing. Polly took my hand. She looked at me. "This is it, Paula. He's ready to go home. Come, take his hand, too."

Oh, boy. The tears started. I couldn't say a word, but Polly started talking to Papa.

"It's all right, Dale. I'm here, and I'll be fine. I want you to go on ahead of me. It won't be long. I'll be with you.

"Be sure to tell your momma and daddy hello for me. I love them.

"And please find our baby Dean (who died in infancy) and hold him for me till I get there.

"When you see my mother and dad, give them a big hug for me and tell them I'm okay.

"Then, please Dale, go down to the water, down where the willows meet the shore and where the grass runs right to the edge of the water, down where the swans swim: I'll meet you there. It won't be long, just a little while. Dale: it's all right. I love you."

She paused. He closed his eyes, and just went on his way. In a few minutes a nurse came in to check his pulse. We smiled as she shook her head. We already knew.

He was gone and for me that was the moment of truth. That moment is the stuff spiritual truth is made from. That moment anchored my spirit to the Rock that will never let me go.

For me, to have known Papa, to see how he lived, to have been with him in that precious moment when he moved to real life, that was the rarest privilege anyone has ever experienced.

How can I express my love and thanksgiving to God for having let me be there? How can I thank him for letting me be with Polly, that tower of strength, in those last moments?

All I can say is that for me the concept of the "Church of God" has withstood the test of time, and I know it will continue to do so for my children and my children's children.

*   *   *

Thank you, Paula. It's an uplifting blessing to know that the faith we read about in the Bible is around today and people like "Dr. Dale" do exist.

If you're looking for a common thread, maybe these ideas will help:

1. The theory of this life as a prelude to eternity is beautiful, but tough to apply when we actually face death.

2. Real love doesn't fade, even in the face of death.

3. Being near solid Christians ministers to us, specially in times of crisis.

4. Sitting apart from real Christian families and observing their lives is inspiring.

5. Choosing between two simultaneous needs is tough; if we allow God to help, God makes it work out for the best.

6. Part of the beauty of heaven will surely be the beautiful citizens who populate it.

7. Once in awhile in our lifetime we feel we almost know how it must have been to stand at the foot of the cross.

One quiet thought to take with you:

"The pilgrimage of this life is but an introduction, a preface, a training school for what is to come."

—Peter Marshall[22]

"Christian: You are on a journey with Jesus. The real purpose of your life now is to stay on that road. Keep learning and never stop. Keep growing and you will want to grow more. Keep praying. Keep reading scripture. Keep on going even when you are tired, discouraged, and feel defeated. Your journey is one of moving ahead and never stopping."
—Oral and Laura Withrow[23]

"We will reap a harvest of
blessing if we don't get discouraged and give in."
—Galatians 6:9,
Living Bible

12

PERSEVERANCE

"There's got to be a way." Ever say that?

Obstacles are opportunities. If no one ever said that someone should. The attitude is not universal but I surely do admire the way many Church of God people have what my mom used to call "stick-to-it-iveness."

Kenneth Crose served in World War II with the Red Cross in Europe and Africa. For those who have served in wartime, you know how tough it usually is to find a Christian in uniform. But Kenneth kept trying. In Persia he finally found Christian fellowship and made the best of not actually finding a Church of God congregation. In Algeria he searched again and again. In desperation, he almost gave up, and then he heard some singing—church music, Christian music. "I haven't the faintest idea what the people were saying in the service, but the music was about Christ. In a few minutes together, the congregation and I identified each other as Christians.

"Perhaps for the first time in my life, I realized what the Church of God meant by reaching our hands in fellowship to all others who are truly Christian."

Down in the Tennessee/Georgia area of our country a giant of a preacher served the Lord faithfully for sixty-two years: John R. Harris. His long service is impressive, but many friends remember best that he was called the "Walking Preacher," for in those sixty-two years of preaching, he never owned a car. He walked or used public transportation. Visiting, touring for revivals, attending camp meetings: he managed it all without a car. That is not easy. That takes stick-to-it-iveness.

What does it take to stick to it?

Gilbert Davila serves with joy and pride among Hispanic peoples. When asked about how he could keep going through the tough times that he endured, his answer was simple: "Some of the great Church of God leaders inspired me." We asked him if any particular ones stood out. "Maurice Caldwell, Nilah Meier Youngman, K.Y. Plank, Don Courtney," he said, and the list goes on. None were our traditional pioneers, no historic names from the past.

"As a teen-ager in Mexico, the modern leaders were very important to me," says Gilbert. "Many local adult leaders whose names you wouldn't recognize were instrumental in my spiritual growth."

As Mark Twain said, erroneous reports often put someone in the grave who later recovers. Flying a modern jet passenger plane is a tremendous responsibility; ask Chauncey Reece about it.

He received a phone call from his home church in Arizona. "Pastor John Denton is deathly ill. We don't know about his chances. Can you help us?" Chauncey asked how he could help.

"Fly in a substitute preacher. Pastor Denton has a special one in mind."

Chauncey did it. Denton recovered and is still going strong. "But," as Chauncey says, "that's no surprise. Pastor John Denton was sent to Arizona nearly thirty years ago because he was about to die. He didn't, and as he preached the gospel, he helped raise up a congregation and led many souls to Christ."

Funny, but when we set our jaws, determined to serve the Lord no matter what, God often sends help to us just when we need it.

Vic Demarest has had a lifetime of discovering encouragers and guides just when he needed them most.

Way back in 1910, way back in the remote village of Coos Bay, Oregon, Vic's parents met, married, and somehow heard of the Church of God. The only person they knew who lived anywhere near them who knew anything about the Church of God was John Neal in Portland.

Vic's family paid Neal's way to come to Coos Bay, where he preached for several weeks. Evidently the gospel of the Church of God that he preached was too much for some of the citizens. "He got the bum's rush out of town" after a few weeks.

An amazing line of Church of God people followed into the lives of the Demarest family. "I can still hear my father's voice as he read from the Bible and prayed," says Vic. A church was established in nearby North Bend and Vic—the eldest—had to help take the family to church each week.

The odyssey continued. A sick mother received prayer from the Gospel Trumpet Company in Anderson, Indiana; she recovered and encouraged Vic to attend Church of God services as a teen-ager. Vic married a Christian girl. Then a terrible accident burned Vic over half his body. The church prayed again.

Time and again dedicated Church of God pastors helped Vic. He shares this trail of spiritual development because he knows God sent people to him each step of the way.

"I learned. I was a slow learner but I learned. My mother taught me, and so did a host of others. My mother's prayers helped me stay the course. I praise God for mother."

Most of us learn sooner or later that what

happens in the long run is what matters. Perseverance makes the difference; surely this is so in the Christian life.

How precious are moments when a saint has passed away and the family of God gathers to celebrate the graduation of someone who has—as Paul put it—"Fought a good fight, . . . finished the course, . . . kept the faith," (2 Tim. 4:7).

How do you remember funerals? Sad, tearful? Yes, but they can also be celebrations. My own dad's funeral included the singing of Handel's "Hallelujah Chorus." At Don Courtney's funeral the congregation sang "Morning Has Broken." There have been tears at such times, but also rejoicing, thankfulness for beautiful lives of testimony and marvelous fellowship that anticipates heaven and reunion with those we love.

The memories that flood in at times like that are quite human, quite common to all families. Barney Warren, one of the Church of God giants in music, often played "creepy mouse" with me when I was young. For the life of me, I can't recall the game, but I remember the fun and the laughter and the warmth of this silver-haired saint.

Pastor Dave Shultz has a similar memory. "I remember that great churchman, Herman Smith, wiggling his ears for me at the dinner table when I was a child."

Perhaps it's this common touch that sometimes inspires children to follow great leaders, and how touching when that leader is in the same family as the children. Pastor Irvin Shrout was such a person. His love of family and his kind and considerate ways must have deeply impressed his sons. They are both ordained pastors and serving in the same congregation: Davis is senior pastor and Martin is the associate pastor. How proud Irvin would be.

Mildred Hatch repeats a story her husband, C. W. Hatch, told again and again. Hatch was reared on a farm, where he and his brothers toiled long and hard in tough times to make a go of it. Hatch's father was a stern, dedicated, go-by-the-rules Christian who was the backbone of their country church in Nebraska.

One Saturday evening the wheat crop was ready to harvest. "Have to wait till Monday. Sunday's God's day," was the word from the head of the household.

"But dad," one of the boys replied, "the weather report says there will be hailstorms Sunday evening. If we wait, we may lose the crop."

Sunday morning the family sat in church as the storm clouds gathered outside. By noon it was black. By sundown the storm had hit and the Hatch wheat crop was lost.

"Dad, if we'd harvested instead of going to church, we'd have wheat in the barn."

Father Hatch smiled. "Yes, but that would be putting God second on God's day. We did right. God comes first."

Mildred smiles now. "Dad Hatch always said, 'I lost a crop, but I saved my boys.' You see, his three sons went into the Church of God ministry and the two girls married ministers."

In the long run persistence pays off—In farming and in families.

The longer we serve Christ, the more we can see God's hand guiding and leading us. Ask Wendell Alison in East Tennessee. Wendell owned and operated a string of bakeries in several cities near the Virginia border. He took daily trips between stores to make sure everything was okay. He worked hard and had little time for Christ or the church.

For some reason on one of his trips he decided to check in with his doctor and see how his general health was. He called ahead and arranged to meet the doctor at a Kingsport, Tennessee, hospital. As the doctor was coming into the hospital Wendell had a massive heart attack. Quickly the staff coordinated their efforts and saved his life.

"You're one lucky man," the doctor said. "If you'd been anywhere else in the area today you'd be a dead man. This hospital has exactly the right staff and equipment to take care of an attack like you had."

In case you're counting, that's miracle number one.

When time came for a six-months checkup, Wendell again went to the Kingsport hospital, met the doctor, and while he was being examined, Wendell suffered a second heart attack. Same results, same summary: You were in the right place at the right time.

Miracle number two.

About this time God really got hold of Wendell. On one trip to the hospital for a checkup, he made up his mind. "I want to be a Christian, a real Christian." But there was no one to pray with him and Wendell wasn't sure what to do. Finally, in desperation, he got out of bed, pulled the backless gown around him and knelt on the floor, away from the door. He prayed, "God, tell me what to do." Wendell says that no sooner had he prayed that sentence than the door opened and a man came in. "Hello, anyone here?" he asked. Wendell stuck his head up.

"Who are you?"

"I'm a pastor and I've come to pray with you."

Without blinking Wendell said, "Fine, come around here and kneel down. I want to give my heart to the Lord."

They knelt; they prayed. Wendell became a Christian, and the pastor left. "Honestly, I don't know who he was. I never saw him before or since." God always comes through.

Miracle number three.

Extensive testing showed that serious heart surgery was needed: the world famous clinic at Cleveland was to be the place. Wendell checked in, went to his room, and started to worry. He'd lost the weight the doctor ordered; he had the best clinic and the best set of doctors. But he was nervous.

Late at night just before surgery Wendell was asleep. He says he woke up with a face appearing in front of his bed. It was a man with a beard. "He looked like Sallman's head of Christ," Wendell said. As he looked, the man spoke. "Boy, you're going to be okay."

Now, no one had called Wendell "boy" for many years. It shocked Wendell and made him remember the incident and the words. But it also brought calm and a good night's sleep.

Surgery went off fine. In the recovery room Wendell recalls slowly waking. In that twilight before he opened his eyes, he felt a hand on his foot and a voice, a very familiar voice from his vision the night before, say, "Boy, you're going to be okay."

Wendell says, "As I opened my eyes, I knew what he would look like. Sure enough, the man with the Sallman face."

Miracle number four.

A year later Wendell returned to Cleveland for a checkup. Calm, almost to boredom, filled him. Late at night, pocket radio quietly playing, Wendell heard a terrible noise in the hall. As he went to the door to see what it was, a man rushed down the hall toward him, suitcase in hand. As he came to Wendell he stopped to complain.

"They put me in here on Friday and now I have to stay all weekend and wait till Monday for surgery. I'm going back to Chicago."

Now, Wendell wasn't much for long conversations, but for some reason he asked the man, "What kind of surgery?" The man described exactly the same surgery as Wendell had had. On an impulse, Wendell asked, "Do you know Christ as your Savior?"

The man, Jewish by birth, looked back in shock. "No, what's that got to do with it?"

Wendell answered without a hesitation. "Well, I had that surgery and it's tough. I'd never do it again if I didn't know Christ and know that he was taking care of me."

The man rushed off in anger, a trail of curses stringing out behind him. But in an hour he was back, knocking on Wendell's door.

"I got to the airport and started onto the plane. Then something said to me, 'You need what that guy back there's got more than you need to go back to Chicago.' How do I get to know this Christ?"

There, on a hospital floor knelt the Tennessee baker and the Chicago Jew. When they arose, both were Christians.

According to Wendell, that's miracle number five. "I don't suppose anyone could have reached that man except one who had been through an operation like he was facing. God put me there." God puts us each where he can use us—if we stick with him, if we keep at it, if we persist. I find many beautiful people in the Church of God who have developed love wrinkles from their long and wonderful walk with our Savior.

I like a church like that.

Can you notice the common theme of these "friends?"

1. Amazing possibilities await us when we stick with it.

2. The simple beliefs that Church of God people hold in common are universal, even when strangers have never heard of any "Church of God."

3. We draw inspiration from leaders who show us what to do and how to do it. People need role models.

4. The Church of God has produced some impressive perseverers.

5. Church of God history sparkles with persecution and unfair treatment. We owe a debt to those who stuck it out.

6. Often our attitudes affect people for Christ far beyond our accomplishments.

7. God still works today. God still calls to us to stay the course.

These friends gave from their hearts:

Oral and Laura Withrow	John R. Harris
Gil Davila	David Shultz
Ken Crose	Wendell Alison
Mildred Hatch	C. W. Hatch
Arnold Harris	Chauncey Reece
John Denton	Vic and Betty Demarest

Something to think about:

"So be glad—yes, actually be glad that you have problems. Be grateful for them as implying that God has confidence in your ability to handle these problems with which he has entrusted you."

—Norman Vincent Peale[24]

"The Church of God: It means a relationship—a relationship with God, made possible through Jesus Christ, a relationship designed to meet people at a point of need."
—Charles R. Shumate[25]

I know this: *I was blind and
now I see.*
—John 9:25, Living Bible

13

CHANGED LIVES

Bob never went to church services. Each
day he'd pass the Church of God building
and keep on going.

Then he heard that the church was planning classes on literacy, classes to teach adults
how to read and write. Bob was an illiterate,
so, gathering all his nerve and overcoming
natural timidity, he stopped in to ask about
the program.

Actually, Bob had never been to school. He
was from a small town in eastern Kentucky
and school attendance laws were neglected
there.

Soon he was involved. He learned quickly and then began to come to the Church of God library to check out books. Someone steered him to the Gospel According to Saint John.

To say the reading and writing were life-changing is but the first step. Bob gave his life to Christ. That was what has made the real difference in his life ever since.

Next, God spoke to Bob about serving. He became a soul-winner. "Did I witness? If you mean did I look around for someone to witness to, then no. I did it the other way around. I asked God to lay on my heart the names of people that he was already speaking to. Then I witnessed to them."

First came Bob's brother, then two drug-addict friends, then a family down the street. Bob describes it:

"Jesus talked to people and he built a relationship between himself and them. Then I added my relationship." He smiles. "I like it that way."

The Church of God believes in life-changing experiences with God. Charles Shumate can vouch for Bob. Learning to read might have been the opening into Bob's spiritual life, but the Church of God has an unending preoccupation with changing the souls and destinies of men and women, boys and girls. To change a life means to change the soul first.

Leroy Falling is a native American who has a heart for the souls of other native Americans. How does today's typical Anglo American reach across cultures to understand and relate to Leroy's people?

Winning souls is vital. Needs are an avenue to touch souls. One well-meaning group of women in Oklahoma wanted to do something to help some of the Navajo women of Klagetoh, Arizona, so they talked it over during one of their regular quilting parties. "Why not pack up several bundles of quilting materials and send them off? Then those wonderful women can have the double joy we have in meeting for fellowship and also getting some quilts made."

As soon as suggested, it was accomplished. Knowing the Navajos were experts in making rugs, the Oklahoma women thought they had better include some quilting instructions. Off went the big bundle of materials for four quilts, with instructions.

Leroy delivered it and waited. One day he got the call, "Come and see the quilt and bring a camera."

When he got there, it took only a moment to convince him there was a misunderstanding somewhere. Two men stood on a pickup and told him to stand back. Then they unfurled the biggest (and most beautiful) quilt Leroy had ever seen. The women had used all four quilt bundles to make one gigantic quilt. "These gals were experts in making rugs; they'd never seen a quilt," said Leroy.

"In that village they still sit around shaking their heads and marveling at the huge beds that those silly Oklahoma women must have."

If you have time you might write or call the Church of God in Fresno and ask about Robbie Jean Brown. She has quite a life-story to tell.

For these pages we'll just say she experienced it all: failure, drugs, immorality of every kind, and suicidal tendencies.

"I hated myself most of my life. Self-esteem was nonexistent. I called on God when I was twenty-four, but I didn't really trust God. Bouts with the devil led to alcohol, drugs, and men; I ended up in a home for alcoholic women."

Loneliness, men who abused her, tranquilizers, sickness, depression, and anger filled her life. She tried "to keep in touch with Jesus" but nothing seemed to work in her life.

"God sent a beautiful woman into my life: Helen Toner. She took me to church with her at the First Church of God in Fresno. When Pastor Williams asked if anyone wanted to pray, I stepped out and my life was changed. I knew that First Church of God was where Jesus wanted me. This is my home. The most loving congregation in my life is there. Helen has opened her life and her home to me. God willing, I'll someday be worthy of all that God and that beautiful woman and her church have done for me."

Changing lives, rescuing Satan's refuse, making sense of the confusion and depression of sin: that's the church; I've found that this is what the Church of God is all about.

"The Church of God has meant salvation to me." That's Ray Houser; pardon me, that's Pastor C. Raymond Houser of Clarksville, Indiana.

He found Christ in the Church of God in Wichita. "At the age of twelve I found the Church of God, or should I say it found me? I loved softball, and twin boys from the Church of God asked me to come and play on their church team. Of course I would. As we practiced day after day, the news came out that if I actually wanted to play in a league game, I'd have to attend church with them. That sounded fair to me. Since I lived near the church building, it was easy, so I attended.

"There I found something different. All my life I'd been in church services. This was different. The kids impressed me. The church family impressed me. They meant what they said. They lived it. In a few weeks I found myself kneeling by my bedside one night and quietly giving my heart to Christ.

"Amazingly, I stuck with it. High school, college, seminary. Then the Church of God ministry. All because one Church of God congregation cared so much for kids that they sponsored a softball team, and all because Don and Ron Smith—now nationally recognized leaders in the Church of God—all because these twins cared enough about me to invite me to come be with them."

Redemption: the saving of that which would otherwise be on the dump heap— that's what the church does.

But it also says, "The church has a need. Can you help?" Be sure to read (in the fourth chapter of John's Gospel) how Jesus did this.

Charley Mills was a carpenter in Seminole, Oklahoma. He didn't attend church much and when he did, the family shopped around at various churches.

One day Pastor Alfred Hammonds stopped Charley in front of the house. "We've purchased a lot for a Church of God building and want to build. But we don't have any money. I have a tough question to ask you. You're a carpenter. Would you help us, without pay, but with a lot of love and appreciation for all you do?"

"Dad wilted," Julia (Mills) Singleton says. "He pitched in to help and soon saw they needed some overall direction in their work. He gave it. He worked his heart out and they got the job done.

"One day, after the building was done, word came that a visiting evangelist, J. D. Harmon, was coming to hold a revival."

"Dad said, 'Hey, let's go see what they're doing in that building we built.' "

"So we went. Mom and dad both gave their lives to Christ. Not many years later the Church of God had a childrens' program. Part of the plan was to include a time for telling about how to be a Christian. Dozens of boys and girls gave their lives to Christ. I was one of them," Julia joyfully says. But she wasn't sure.

Julia wrestled with what being a Christian

was. One day—just twelve years old at the time—she bowed in her bedroom, just before going to school. "Outside my window a bird was singing. I knew I wanted Christ. So I said, 'I claim Jesus; maybe I'll understand later all this means.' In that moment my life was Christ's. My heart sang as the bird's heart was doing out there in the yard."

Her testing came quickly. That very morning in school Julia bumped into the one girl in the class whom she hated. "I had been thinking about her and how I felt. When I bumped into her, I loved her. Jesus really does change people."

My, how a small event can change lives. "Shall we include Sapulpa, Oklahoma on our schedule this year?" the Christian Brotherhood Hour quartet was discussing. They decided to do it.

That one concert was the deciding factor in Ron Patty's plans for college. He was drawn to the University of Oklahoma and their great football program. Ron was a top quarterback. But he also loved music.

Ron went to the Church of God college in Anderson, Indiana. There he met Carolyn Tunnel, a young woman, by the way, whose home church in California had also been on the quartet's schedule. They fell in love, married, and had three children who love music: Mike, Craig, and the one and only Sandi Patti. If the quartet had decided otherwise, who knows?

By the way, Ron keeps his love of sports. In case you hadn't heard, he pitched baseball in college. After their wedding ceremony, Ron and Carolyn headed for the diamond where Carolyn waited patiently as Ron pitched both ends of a doubleheader for Anderson College (and won them both).

Changed lives is what the church is all about. And those changes come in all shapes and sizes.

For lots of Church of God people Warner Press is the place where Church of God materials are published. "For me," says Gertrude Springer Popp, "it's the place where I found Christ. When I was just a tot the old Gospel Trumpet family had worship services in a chapel." There Christ came into her life. "That service so long ago was the highlight of my love for the Church of God." Writing, printing, mailing: the whole scheme of getting the printed word out also has the personal, inner concern of the people involved.

Cisco, Texas, isn't much of a metropolis. It never has been. When Leta Jefford was a little girl in Cisco, she lived near a beautiful white church with a tall steeple and the friendliest people she'd ever known. It sort of prejudiced her in favor of churches and what they stood for.

The family moved away from Cisco. Leta grew, married, and kept moving—back and forth until Leta and her own growing family settled in Sacramento. Soon they were attending a marvelous Church of God congregation there. "Friendly, loving, just like I imagined everyone was in my dream church back in Cisco. You know, I never went inside that little white church when I was a child, but the Church of God in Sacramento seemed like an adult fulfillment of my childhood fantasies about churches.

"Then one day I was working in the church office. I spotted a Church of God yearbook. I looked up Cisco. To my unbounded astonishment I discovered that the little white dream church of my childhood had been a Church of God congregation."

With a tear, she sums it up: "I think God used the Church of God to get my heart ready for a time when I could find Christ and really get my life in order. I love the Church of God."

No wonder. I love it, too. I love what God does through the Church of God to redeem, save, change, and transform.

It means the world to me.

Changed lives often mean working where there is a need, without restrictions, without preconceived notions. Ask Helen Durham Russell about ministry and she'll tell you.

Reared in a "small town, under a strict mother and strict pastor," she found Christ as her Savior and served him well. It was a special commitment. "I gave him the rest of my life. For God I'll live. For God I'll die."

Significant ministry began with a 1964 call

as a lay minister; a few years later this developed into a radio ministry. The next step was tougher: a prison ministry. Being a "pastor to prisoners" began with six people in the basement, including a blind accordianist. "God helped us get a building and today we're moving ahead."

The crowds are larger and so is the ministry—radio, the homeless, the prisons, the derelicts, and a sprinkling of legislators. By the way, Pastor Russell ministers in five penal institutions in Maryland, to senior citizens, drug addicts, and alcoholics. But she's also the first black woman ever to lead the U.S. Congress in prayer.

The Church of God means working with God, in a relationship, to change lives.

That's what the Church of God means to my friends and me.

That's what the Church of God can mean to you, too, if you're interested in something vital, something worth tackling in a world such as ours.

My friends and I feel strongly about experience and change:

1. Lives can be changed for the better by Jesus Christ, today, right where each of us live.

2. People have needs. Christians in the Church of God who genuinely care show that concern by responding to those needs.

3. When people find something that fulfills a need, they delight in spreading the news.

4. God works through the church to speak to the souls of people.

5. Most people detect, understand, and respond to Christians who are living what they are preaching.

6. At its best the Church of God concerns itself about souls.

7. Many people across the country and around the world have a love affair going with the Church of God, many times because that's where they found Jesus Christ.

8. God works through the church, entrusting people with ministries that touch souls.

These friends contributed to this chapter:

Jill and Brandon King
Robbie Lee Brown
C. Raymond and Tina Houser
Gertrude Singer Popp
Julia Mills Singleton
Helen Durham Russell

Leroy Falling
Morris Williams
Charley Mills
Alfred Hammons
Leta Jefford
Charles R. Shumate

From the mouth of a member of the church:

"The Church of God is where you can pray and talk about accepting the Lord. It is a way to ask Jesus into your heart. Then people can get baptized."

—Brandon King, age 12[26]

GO WHERE THE FAITH IS

Well, that's how I feel about the Church of God; and, as you can see, lots of others feel strongly and positively about the church.

Sam Shoemaker—a great Christian who seemed to be a real believer in the spirit and message of the Church of God—said something about people always asking him for faith. He told them if they wanted knowledge, they should know to go to school. So if they wanted faith, they should go to the place where faith-filled people were: they should go to church.

You can study about the Church of God; you can take the word of my friends and me; you can read expert opinions on the matter.

But nothing will satisfy like attending a service at the nearest Church of God place of worship. Go where the church meets.

When you do, you may very well bump into someone who has had a miraculous experience of healing or been touched by God in some other marvelous way.

In case you want to follow up on the messages we've shared in these pages, we have included a couple of extra sections at the end of the book. Most of the authors and most of the people in the offices listed are wonderful people, people worth knowing. As we've been saying, this Church of God is a family, and all the members of it are special.

We'd love to include you in the ever expanding clan.

SPECIAL THANKS

At the close of each chapter are lists of persons who contributed directly to some specific part of that chapter. Listed below are a number of friends who sent marvelous stories, ideas, personal experiences, and testimonies. Most of these are found in one form or another in these pages. But in case I haven't noted the exact contribution, I list my friends and say a big, public "thank you" for your help, your inspiration, and, especially, for your deep feelings about the Church of God.

Phyllis Matzigkiet Dobson, Santa Cruz, Mexico

Jo Sommer, Scio, OR

M. Grosvenor, Moscow, ID

Glenn Miller, Bluefield, VA

Richard D. Collins, Erice, ND

JoAnn Chestnut, Tuttle, OK

Evelyn Alison, Piney Flats, TN

Sawak Sarju, Surrey, BC, Canada

Craig Frank, Lake Wales, FL

Myrtle Kennedy, Salt Lick, KY

Marcia Howland, Houston, TX

Mettie Starkey, Hermitage, TN

Orville Easterling, WV

IF YOU'D LIKE TO KNOW MORE . . .

There are some addresses you should know about:

The Executive Council of the Church of God, Box 2420, Anderson, IN 46018.
- Information on the Church of God from the central coordinating office of the Church of God.

The Board of Church Extension and Home Missions, Box 2069, Anderson, IN 46018.
- Information about investments, evangelism, missions work within the U.S., and help for local congregations in the fields of finance, planning for the future, and planting other churches.

The Board of Christian Education, Box 2458, Anderson, IN 46018-2458.
- Information on leadership development, family life, and Christian education ministries.

Mass Communications Board, Box 2007, Anderson, IN 46018.
- Information on media sharing of the gospel around the world.

Missionary Board, Box 2498, Anderson, IN 46018.
- Information on evangelism outreach ministries beyond the United States and Canada.

Missions Education, Box 2337, Anderson, IN 46018
- Information on the missionary projects of

the Church of God around the world; primarily the publisher of *Church of God Missions* magazine.

Women of the Church of God, Box 2328, Anderson, IN 46018-2328.
- Information on womens' ministries and activities, both within the local congregation and among the congregations.

Commission on Christian Higher Education, Box 2420, Anderson, IN, 46018.
- Information on the Bible colleges, seminary, and other colleges sponsored by the Church of God.

Warner Press, Box 2499, Anderson, IN 46018.
- Information on publications, books, periodicals, and Sunday school materials available. Toll free #(800) 347-6468.

IF YOU'D LIKE TO READ MORE ABOUT THE CHURCH OF GOD

Let me recommend these books and periodicals to you. Unless otherwise indicated, they are available from Warner Press, Box 2499, Anderson, IN 46018; I'd recommend also that you call and ask about those that interest you: (800) 347-6468 (toll-free call).

Periodicals:

Vital Christianity, the official family periodical for the Church of God; published monthly.

Church of God Missions magazine, published monthly by the Missions Education department, Box 2337, Anderson, IN 46018.

Pathways to God, a daily devotional magazine, published quarterly with devotions for each day of the year.

"Journey With the Word" Sunday school materials. Excellent for personal study.

Film: For groups and families wanting to see an excellent historical panorama of the Church of God, Warner Press rents "Heaven to Earth" video. Also available for rent in 16 mm. film.

Books:

(1) General books to tell you what the Church of God is all about

A Look at the Church of God (Vol. I, II) Two fine photo-filled books; written for children, but finding favor with a large number of adults wanting an easy-to-read story of the Church of God. (Hardback, large size, about $10 each)

A Brief History of the Church of God, by John W. V. Smith. Great paperback overview of our past.

Meet Me at the Cross, a small paperback introduction to the Church of God; wonderful for giving to people who show interest. (about 50¢ each)

Basics for Belief, a paperback general look at the teachings of the Church of God. (About $2.)

(2) Other books about the Church of God, looking at particular areas of concern that we have shown

I Will Build My Church, paperback, about $4.

The First Century (2 vol. history), hardback, set $20.

Passport for a Reformation (missions), hardback, about $8.

Walking in Missionary Shoes, hardback, $15.

The Church of God As Revealed in Scripture, paperback, about $2; excellent for Bible introduction to the Church of God; good for group study.

Quest for Holiness and Unity, hardback, about $17.

(3) Books that interpret doctrine and scripture; good for insights into the Church of God, but also good for general Bible study: individual and groups. Priced between $1.50 and $6.

This We Believe, Martin.

Healing and Wholeness, Sterner.

The Life of Salvation, Stafford

Two, briefer and less expensive: *The Gifts of*

the Spirit, by Blackwelder, 35; 2 vol. *Christian Theology* by Gray, $1.50 each.
The Word of God, Jones.
God's Caring People, Sterner.
The Bible and Today's Tongues, Bradley.
Receive the Holy Spirit, Newell.
This Glorious Church, Lawrence.
Commitment to Holiness, Jones.
Concerning Christian Unity, Massey.
Two, larger, more detailed, hard back: *The Wesleyan Theological Perspective* (5 vol. $14.95 each, $69.50 for the set) *Christian Theology*, Byrum, $14.95.
Family Reunion: A Century of Camp Meetings, Willowby.

Remember, each month new material is being published by many of the agencies listed. A call to Warner Press will answer your questions: (800) 347-6468.

Notes on the Quotes

1. James Earl Massey, *The Responsible Pulpit* (Anderson, IN: Warner Press, 1974).

2. Inez Cobb, Porterville, CA, private correspondence.

3. Edwin Markham, "Quatrain" from *1000 Quotable Poems* (New York: Bonanza Books, 1985).

4. Holly Miller, "Gaithers Discover 'The Family of God' Begins at Home" in *Vital Christianity* (Anderson, IN: Warner Press, 20 September 1987).

5. Herbert Brokering, "Prayer of Dedication," from *Lord, Be With Us* (St. Louis: Concordia Publishing House, 1969).

6. Kenneth L. Crose, Anderson, IN, private correspondence.

7. Omar Bradley, address, Armistice Day, 1948 from *The Great Thoughts* (New York: Ballentine Books, 1985), 49.

8. Helen Durham Russell, Baltimore, MD, private correspondence.

9. G. K. Chesterton, "What's Wrong With the World" from *The Great Thoughts* (New York: Ballentine Books, 1985), 78.

10. Merle Strege, "Parents' Duties to Their Children" in *Vital Christianity* (Anderson, IN: Warner Press, 11 January 1987).

11. H. M. Riggle, *The New Testament Church* (Anderson, IN: The Gospel Trumpet Co., 1937).

12. Sara Lindemuth, "Caring Enough to Help" in *Vital Christianity* (Anderson, IN: Warner Press, 11 January 1987).

13. Alexander Solzhenitsyn, "Assurance"

from *Solzhenitsyn: A Pictorial Autobiography* (New York: Farrar, Atraus and Giroux, 1974).

14. Maurice Berquist, *The Miracle and Power of Blessing* (Anderson, IN: Warner Press, 1983).

15. Frances Benfield, Johnson City, TN, private correspondence.

16. Jack Hobson, Fresno, CA, private correspondence.

17. Kathryn Ann Lindskoog, "True Charity," from C. S. Lewis, *Mere Christianity* (Glendale, CA: Gospel Light Publishers, 1973).

18. Harold Phillips, *Knowing the Living God* (Anderson, IN: Warner Press, 1968).

19. Sidney Lanier, "The Marshes of Glynn," from *Favorite Inspirational Poems* (Old Tappan, NJ: Fleming H. Revel Co., 1960).

20. Martin Luther King, Jr., speech, June 23, 1963, from *The Great Thoughts* (New York: Ballentine Books, 1985).

21. Gilbert W. Stafford, "Broadcasting the Gospel," in *Vital Christianity* (Anderson, IN: Warner Press, 25 January 1987).

22. Peter Marshall, "Liberation from Materialism," from *The Prayers of Peter Marshall*, edited by Catherine Marshall (New York: McGraw-Hill, 1954).

23. Oral and Laura Withrow, *Welcome to the Family* (Anderson, IN: Warner Press, 1989).

24. Norman Vincent Peale, "Problems," from *Positive Thinking for a Time Like This* (Englewood Cliffs, NJ: Prentice-Hall, 1975).

25. Charles Shumate, Anderson, IN, private correspondence.

26. Brandon King, Madrid, IA, private correspondence.